Jurists and Judges

An Essay on Influence

NEIL DUXBURY

OXFORD – PORTLAND OREGON
2001

Hart Publishing
Oxford and Portland, Oregon

Published in North America (US and Canada) by
Hart Publishing c/o
International Specialized Book Services
5804 NE Hassalo Street
Portland, Oregon
97213-3644
USA

Distributed in the Netherlands, Belgium and Luxembourg by
Intersentia, Churchillaan 108
B2900 Schoten
Antwerpen
Belgium

Hart Publishing is a specialist legal publisher based in Oxford, England.
To order further copies of this book or to request a list of other publications please write to:

Hart Publishing, Salter's Boatyard, Folly Bridge,
Abingdon Road, Oxford OX1 4LB
Telephone: +44 (0)1865 245533 or Fax: +44 (0)1865 794882
e-mail: mail@hartpub.co.uk
WEBSITE: http//www.hartpub.co.uk

British Library Cataloguing in Publication Data
Data Available
ISBN 1–84113–204–7 (paperback)

Typeset by Hope Services (Abingdon) Ltd.
Printed and bound in Great Britain on acid-free paper by
Biddles Ltd, www.biddles.co.uk

To

M. L. & A. I. O.

Influences

Preface

This book is an attempt to muddy waters. Essentially an article with delusions of grandeur, it revolves around a point which is perhaps as unhelpful as it is specific. The point might be stated thus: the familiar argument that juristic speculation in England has been largely uninfluential as compared with similar pursuits elsewhere is often presented in an inordinately simplistic fashion. While the argument might be correct, its correctness is too often taken for granted. A few cross-jurisdictional comparisons reveal that assertions about the relatively uninfluential status of English academic lawyers invariably turn out to be questionable.

Much has been made of the failures of English legal academics. Accounts of the development of academic law in England tend to present the jurist as unable either to exert much influence on the profession or to make a favourable intellectual impression on the wider academic world. In one way or another this jurist often seems variously angry, insecure, frustrated, resentful, or even resigned to what he (for it usually is a he) sees as his place in the scheme of things. From these accounts, however, there seems to be something missing. In short, too little is made of the ways in which academic lawyers have proved influential. There exists a long and rich history of jurists influencing the development of English law. While this particular book attempts to elaborate a specific point—summarized in the preceding paragraph—about influence, it is really only a prelude to the far more formidable project of unravelling and explaining the general history. Numerous valuable contributions to that project already exist, and I hope to make some contributions of my own in the future. Before endeavouring to do so, however, it seemed to make sense to get this particular essay out of my system, since I suspect that it is the backdrop to some of the other studies which I plan to undertake.

In preparing this book, I have benefited considerably from research support provided by the Institute of Advanced Legal Studies, London, where I currently hold a non-residential visiting fellowship. I am grateful to those people who commented on presentations of this project at the Institute and at the law faculties of Emory University, the University of Manchester, the University of Newcastle, the University of Southampton, Vanderbilt University and the University of Virginia. The project has also been improved by help and feedback which I have received from Jean-Bernard Auby, Jack Balkin, John Bell, Brian Bix, David Booton, Margot Brazier, Roger Brownsword, Hazel Carty, Rob Cryer, Martin Davey, Marie Fox, Peter Goodrich, Andrew Halpin, Tony Honoré, Tony Jolowicz, Gareth Jones, Kirsty Keywood, Matthew Kramer, Nicola Lacey, Martin Loughlin, Anthony Ogus, Richard Posner, Mike Redmayne, Ben Richardson, Jack Schlegel, Robert Stevens, David Sugarman, Robert Thomas, Martin Wasik and Ted White.

Manchester
17 October 2000

Contents

1. Introduction 1

2. The Dynamics of Influence 5
   Citation and its significance 8
   The elusiveness of influence 17

3. The USA 23
   Judges on scholarship 24
   Academics on scholarship 33
   What is to be done? 38

4. France 47
   History of the note d'arrêt 48
   Case notes and influence 54

5. England 61
   The value of death 62
   Silver linings 77
      Better read when dead? 78
      Pollock, Goodhart and case notes 84
   Modern times 101
   Conclusion 113

6. Envoi 117

Index 119

1

Introduction

TO WHAT EXTENT do judges take account of legal scholarship? In English law, there exists a fairly large body of literature which—more often than not—answers this question in a not especially sanguine fashion. Although many modern accounts of legal scholarship in England indicate that academics are not without influence and that, over the past century, the gap between jurist and judge narrowed significantly, there is still a tendency for commentators on the English scene to believe that the grass must be greener elsewhere. On the continent and across the Atlantic, to paraphrase a familiar refrain, academic lawyers are clearly held in higher regard than they are in England.[1] "I feel it is rather forgiving of you to invite judges, or indeed any type of practical lawyer", commented one eminent English judge in his address to the Society of Public Teachers of Law in 1958, "because when you compare the status of the academic lawyer in most other systems of law he is very much more honoured and more reverence is paid to him than there is in this country".[2] To this refrain there is no doubt a considerable amount of truth. It is probably also the case, however, that the refrain oversimplifies the picture. When assessments are made concerning the influence of scholarship on courts from one jurisdiction to the next, after all, what might be the appropriate criteria of comparison? The predisposition of judges towards citation of academic commentary—to take what is perhaps the most obvious comparator—is likely to be a useful measure of influence. Yet we may overvalue citation. Citations to a work of scholarship are not necessarily indicative of its influence, just as absence of citation to that work does not compel the conclusion that it has had no influence. In jurisdiction A, where judges regularly refer to scholarship, citation of a

[1] For instances of the refrain see, e.g., P. S. Atiyah, *Pragmatism and Theory in English Law* (London, Stevens & Sons, 1987), pp.38–42; R. C. van Caenegem, *Judges, Legislators and Professors: Chapters in European Legal History* (Cambridge, Cambridge University Press, 1987), pp.53–65; and note also W. L. Twining, "Goodbye to Lewis Eliot: The Academic Lawyer as Scholar" (1980) n.s. 15 *J.S.P.T.L.* 2.

[2] Patrick Devlin, "Statutory Offences" (1958) n.s. 4 *J.S.P.T.L.* 206; repr. in his *Samples of Lawmaking* (London, Oxford University Press, 1962), pp.67–82 at 67.

work is likely to prove a decent proxy for its influence upon the courts. In jurisdiction B, where judicial resort to the writings of academics has for one reason or another been discouraged, study of citation is unlikely to prove especially revealing. This does not necessarily mean that in jurisdiction B the work of academics has generally had no impact on the courts. It indicates, rather, that for the purpose of assessing judicial attitudes to scholarship in jurisdiction B, citation is unlikely to be a useful measure of influence. Properly to assess the influence of scholarship on courts in jurisdiction B requires an exercise different from that which is most appropriate for estimating influence in jurisdiction A.

Discussions about different judicial estimations of scholarship from one jurisdiction to the next seem generally to miss this point. It may well be correct to assert that in France, "university professors have generally a much more respected status than seems to be the case in England",[3] or that whereas "leading American law schools have had a great influence on the American legal order . . . English law schools have a negligible impact on the English legal order".[4] But might it not be the case that in England qualities such as respect and influence are simply manifested differently than they are in France and the USA? Is it not possible that there exists here a problem of incommensurability? If, from one jurisdiction to the next, academic influence rears its head in different ways, what are we comparing?

This book considers the impact of juristic opinion on the courts in the USA, France and England.[5] The thesis of the book is *not* that comparative lawyers have been wrong to argue that continental and American academic lawyers have been more successful in influencing judicial thought than have English academic lawyers. It would be very surprising if this argument were not correct. What this book *does* claim, however, is that the comparisons to be made are not straight-

[3] John Bell, Sophie Boyron and Simon Whittaker, *Principles of French Law* (Oxford, Oxford University Press, 1998), p.36.

[4] P. S. Atiyah and Robert S. Summers, *Form and Substance in Anglo-American Law: A Comparative Study of Legal Reasoning, Legal Theory, and Legal Institutions* (Oxford, Clarendon Press, 1987), pp.403–4.

[5] In this study I use the term "jurist" as if it were synonymous with terms such as "academic lawyer", "legal academic" and "university lawyer". Perhaps in doing so I rather belittle the notion of jurist, which has particularly grandiose connotations. For historical accounts which, with good reason, exalt the figure of the jurist, see Roscoe Pound, *Interpretations of Legal History* (Cambridge, Cambridge University Press, 1923), pp.116–40; and Carleton Kemp Allen, *Law in the Making* (3rd edn., Oxford, Clarendon Press, 1939), pp.110–15.

forward owing to the fact that, within each of these jurisdictions, influence takes a different form. By endeavouring to outline some of the dynamics of influence I hope to show that academic commentary in particular jurisdictions sometimes turns out to be more influential, and occasionally less influential, than has commonly been assumed.

Chapter 2 is a short essay on the complexity of influence. Chapters 3, 4 and 5 examine the impact of juristic opinion on judicial thought in each of the countries under consideration. The main focus of the project is juristic influence in England: thus it is that Chapter 5 comprises almost half the book. Other jurisdictions might usefully have been studied: in countries such as Germany and Australia, to name but two examples, legal scholarship can be seen to have had considerable influence on judicial thinking.[6] Not only is the focus of this study limited to three jurisdictions, but it examines the influence of academic commentary only on judicial thought rather than on the development of law in general. In attempting to assess the relationship between the work of the law schools and the work of the courts in the USA, the basis of my approach has been to look at what academics and judges have had to say about that relationship. With regard to France and England, the analyses emphasize a particular type of (mainly academic) legal commentary—the so-called case note—the like of which is not much in evidence in the USA.

All things considered, my approach is quite narrow. I hope, however, that it is satisfactory for the task which I have set myself; for the point of this book is not to offer a general account of the impact of scholarship on the courts but to demonstrate the chameleon character of influence and to argue that, because legal scholarship can be influential for numerous reasons (and because the reasons for the influence of scholarship vary from one context to the next), we should always be wary about making general comparative statements concerning judicial regard for legal scholarship as between jurisdictions.

[6] For relevant discussions see, e.g., Sir Anthony Mason, "The Tort Law Review" (1993) 1 *Tort Law Rev*. 5; Hein Kötz, "Scholarship and the Courts: A Comparative Survey", in D. S. Clark (ed.), *Comparative and Private International Law: Essays in Honor of John Henry Merryman on his Seventieth Birthday* (Berlin, Duncker & Humblot, 1990), pp. 183–95 at 193–4; and B. S. Markesinis, "A Matter of Style" (1994) 110 *L.Q.R.* 607 at 609.

2

The Dynamics of Influence

INFLUENCE CONCERNS THE effects of one thing upon another. Following its derivation from the Latin *influere*, we might say that influence comes about where something from A flows into and thereby affects B.[1] Landes and Posner identify influence thus: A has influenced B if it is the case that, had A never existed, B would either be different from what it now is, or—because A was not present to accelerate change—would have taken longer to become what it now is.[2] The difficulty with this conceptualization of influence is that it assumes the idea to be more closely bound up with the notion of causality than is necessarily the case. Certain instances which fall within Landes's and Posner's conceptualization concern not influence but causality. If B were to be assaulted and paralyzed by A, for example, B would obviously be different from what he now is, but it would be odd to claim here that A had influenced B. (Likewise, we can identify instances which concern not causality but influence: A might inspire B's course of action, for example, but not necessarily cause it.)[3] Posner has recently refined his conceptualization of influence in order to accommodate the fact that the notion can entail both cause ("the situation in which B would not have used the idea if A had never held it") and inspiration ("the situation in which . . . an idea . . . is picked up *from* A by B

[1] On the etymology of influence, see Ronald Primeau, "Introduction", in R. Primeau (ed.), *Influx: Essays on Literary Influence* (Port Washington, N.Y., Kennikat Press, 1977), pp. 3–12 at 5–6.

[2] William M. Landes and Richard A. Posner, "The Influence of Economics on Law: A Quantitative Study" (1993) 36 *J. Law & Econ*. 385 at 385–6.

[3] Thus, although the television programme, "L.A. Law", might have been an inspiration for many Americans who have decided to pursue legal careers, it is unlikely that the programme *caused* many of those people to become lawyers: see Charles B. Rosenberg, "An *L.A. Lawyer* Replies" (1989) 98 *Yale L. J*. 1625 at 1627. Of course, the dividing line between A's inspiring and A's causing B's course of action may sometimes be quite narrow: while it may be an overstatement to say that film violence actually causes some people to harm others, or that photographs of extremely slim fashion models cause some impressionable people to become anorexic or even that advertising causes individual consumers to choose certain brands over others, the language of causality does not seem too far out of place in relation to such issues and it is not altogether surprising to find that debates centred around them sometimes treat influence and cause as synonymous.

and used by B").[4] This refinement might itself benefit from elaboration: the state of being inspired—of B's picking up an idea from A—is not necessarily a conscious one: sometimes, that is, we are influenced by past experiences without being aware of the fact.[5] Influence, then, is related but not identical to causality: it occurs where a person's outlook alters as a result of his or her conscious or subconscious noticing of some external stimulus.

Of course, it may be hard or even impossible to ascertain that a person's outlook has changed owing to their having consciously or subconsciously noticed some external stimulus. In the absence of A, perhaps B would have become what he now is anyway, owing to the existence of C (or D, or E, etc.). Not only might other phenomena have contributed to B becoming what he now is, but it may be impossible for us to ascertain what B would have been like had A not existed. Showing that A has influenced B can be difficult; showing that A has had a *unique* influence on B might be even more of a problem.

The elusiveness of influence is something with which literary theorists in particular have long tried to grapple. Within literary theory, influence has traditionally been conceived to be the process whereby ideas, themes, preoccupations or whatever flow from one literary work into another, thereby affecting the latter.[6] But this notion of influence has proved especially problematic. Some apparent literary influences may in fact be coincidental resemblances. Some influences may not be wholly or even partly attributable to other literary works: many things other than literature may influence an author.[7] Some influences, furthermore, resist identification or disaggregation. T. S. Eliot was influenced by Ezra Pound. Ezra Pound was influenced by Robert Browning. Eliot, although he read Browning, professed not to have

[4] Richard A. Posner, "Bentham's Influence on the Law and Economics Movement" (1998) 51 *Current Legal Problems* 425 at 426.

[5] On the phenomenon of implicit memory, see Daniel L. Schacter, *Searching for Memory: The Brain, The Mind, and the Past* (New York, Basic Books, 1996), pp.161–91.

[6] See, e.g., Claudio Guillén, "The Aesthetics of Literary Influence", in Primeau, *supra* n. 1, pp.49–73 at 58: "An influence, according to the old nineteenth-century idea, was the transfer and rearrangement of literary forms and themes from one work to another".

[7] "What precisely do we mean when we say that a certain writer has been the object of a demonstrable influence? Presumably we mean that he has been affected by some other writer in a particular way. But then, authors are affected by a great many things which become part of their vast hoard of experience; they are affected by a sunset or the loss of a daughter, addiction to a drug or a love affair . . . The notion of an affective power is therefore too vague to throw much light on the concept of literary influences": Ihab H. Hassan, "The Problem of Influence in Literary History: Notes Towards a Definition" (1955) 14 *Jnl. of Aesthetics & Art Criticism* 66 at 67.

been influenced by him. The degree to which the Browningesque traits in Eliot's poetic technique might be traced—notwithstanding his own disclaimer—to his reading of Browning and how much to his indebtedness to Pound is a matter about which we can only speculate. (A third possibility, which does not exclude the other two, is that Eliot's use of the dramatic monologue and of colloquial diction is evidence of Browning's influence upon poetic technique in general during the early decades of the twentieth century.)[8] Of course, the identification of specific literary influences will not always be a speculative exercise: just as we can assert with confidence that Pound influenced Eliot, so too we might assert that Ruskin influenced Proust or that Wordsworth influenced Shelley. But since the identification of influences frequently does entail speculation, literary theorists often argue that such an exercise has little to commend it.[9]

That literary theorists should have been both intrigued and confounded by influence is understandable. For many scholars of literature, one imagines, few things are as likely to raise the adrenalin as the prospect of demonstrating the existence of some previously unestablished or, better still, unsuspected literary influence.[10] The reason for this is that it is often very difficult, as we have already noted, to demonstrate (rather than merely speculate about) literary influences, not least because novelists and poets rarely acknowledge their sources of inspiration.[11] To some extent, courts are comparable: it is often the case, that is, that judges do not attribute their reasoning to the source that inspired it. But it is important not to stretch this comparison too far. With regard to influence, and in comparison with literary works, judicial decisions can be more transparent: judges, certainly within the common law tradition, often will identify the sources which have motivated their reasoning. Rarely can we identify influences on a novelist or poet by considering what he or she has cited, for novelists and poets do not conventionally cite anything; judges, by contrast, do make use of citation—even if (as is sometimes the case) they only cite the decisions of other judges.

[8] See Richard D. Altick, *The Art of Literary Research* (rev. edn., New York, Norton, 1975), p.112.

[9] See, e.g., Hassan, *supra* n. 7, *passim*; Haskell M. Block, "The Concept of Influence in Comparative Literature" (1958) 7 *Yearbook of Comparative & General Literature* 30.

[10] Consider, in this regard, David Lodge, *Small World: An Academic Romance* (Harmondsworth, Penguin, 1985 [1984]), pp.51–2.

[11] When they do acknowledge such sources, furthermore, the effort often serves to render the notion of influence yet more labyrinthine: see, e.g., Nicholson Baker, *U and I: A True Story* (London, Granta, 1991).

CITATION AND ITS SIGNIFICANCE

As a method of identifying instances in which scholarship has had an influence on courts, the study of citations will sometimes yield little fruit owing to the fact that some courts have traditionally adhered to conventions which militate against the citation of academic commentary. While, for example, Article 38(1)(d) of the Statute of the International Court of Justice permits the Court to apply "the teachings of the most highly qualified publicists of the various nations, as subsidiary means for the determination of rules of law", and while the International Court is likely to make use of such teachings, they are rarely referred to in the majority judgments owing to the process of collective drafting of such judgments and the desire to avoid invidious selection of citations.[12] This is not to deny that citations will often provide a useful means of identifying instances where judges have been influenced by academics. The identification and the assessment of influence are two very different exercises, however, and the limitations of citation analysis usually become most evident not when we are trying to locate influence but when we are trying to measure it.

Law is by no means as obsessed with citation analysis as are certain other disciplines.[13] Legal writing, nevertheless, is commonly reliant on citations—particularly to legal sources—and so is fairly well suited to such analysis.[14] The basic premise of citation analysis is that documents cited frequently are likely to be more influential than those

[12] See Ian Brownlie, *Principles of Public International Law* (5th edn., Oxford, Oxford University Press, 1998), pp.24–5. The use of the works of commentators is more likely to be evident from the dissenting and separate opinions in which the "workings" of individual judges are set out in more detail. References to the works of commentators are also likely to be found in the pleadings before the Court: Brownlie, *ibid.*, p.25. See further Mohamed Shahabuddeen, *Precedent in the World Court* (Cambridge, Cambridge University Press, 1996), pp.203–8.

[13] Although scientists tend to be considerably more preoccupied with citation analysis than are lawyers, it has been argued in the USA that law is in fact the birthplace of citation study: see Fred R. Shapiro, "Origins of Bibliometrics, Citation Indexing, and Citation Analysis: The Neglected Legal Literature" (1992) 43 *J. Am. Soc. for Info. Science* 337.

[14] Perhaps the primary example of such analysis in a legal context is Shapiro's work on citation hierarchies in American law reviews: see Fred R. Shapiro, "The Most-Cited Law Review Articles" (1985) 73 *Calif. L. Rev.* 1540; *The Most-Cited Law Review Articles* (Buffalo, N.Y., Hein, 1987) (anthology of the most-cited articles); "The Most-Cited Articles from *The Yale Law Journal*" (1991) 100 *Yale L. J.* 1449; "The Most-Cited Law Review Articles Revisited" (1996) 71 *Chicago-Kent L. Rev.* 751; "The Most-Cited Law Reviews" (2000) 29 *J. Leg. Studs.* 389.

which are cited less frequently, and therefore the impact of a particular document can be estimated by counting the number of occasions on which it has been cited. Citation, in short, might be treated as a proxy for influence.

Before examining the relationship between citation and influence, it is worthwhile considering the various possible motivations for citation.[15] Sometimes the primary purpose of citation is to identify sources of information which enable the reader to verify the accuracy of the writer's statements. Grafton has argued that, for historians, footnotes are a "rough equivalent of the scientist's report on data . . . Historical footnotes list not the great writers who sanction a given statement or whose words an author has creatively adapted, but the documents . . . which provided its substantive ingredients".[16] Another type of citation is that with which Grafton purports not to be concerned in the above quotation: one may hold a particular view and, in an effort to enhance the credibility of that view, seek out sources which back it up. Some citations are intended not so much to verify or enhance the credibility of a statement as to direct the reader to information relevant to that statement or simply to give credit to related work. Others are intended to demonstrate compliance with norms against plagiarism.[17] Citations may be negatively oriented, identifying works with which the writer disagrees.[18] Slightly different are those citations which are intended to differentiate one's product from that which has been produced by others: while others have claimed X—cue citation—I am claiming X + Y.[19] Slightly different again is the phenomenon of "power-citing", a

[15] There is a massive body of literature addressing such motivations. For a general survey see Blaise Cronin, *The Citation Process: The Role and Significance of Citations in Scientific Communication* (London, Taylor Graham, 1984), pp.50–73.

[16] Anthony Grafton, *The Footnote: A Curious History* (Cambridge, Mass., Harvard University Press, 1997), pp.vii, 33. In a similar vein, see Peter Novick, *That Noble Dream: The "Objectivity Question" and the American Legal Profession* (Cambridge, Cambridge University Press, 1988), p.220 fn. 25.

[17] See further Richard A. Posner, *The Theory and Practice of Citations Analysis, with Special Reference to Law and Economics* (University of Chicago Law School, John M. Olin Law & Economics Working Paper No. 83 (2d ser.), September 1999), p.5, available at <http://www.law.uchicago.edu/Publications/Working/index.html>.

[18] Coase has noted in relation to his widely-cited article, "The Problem of Social Cost", that "[m]any of the citations in the economics literature are in fact articles attacking my views": R. H. Coase, "The Problem of Social Cost: The Citations" (1996) 71 *Chicago-Kent L. Rev.* 809 at 810. It is tempting to apply such a statement in support of the claim that citations do not easily translate into influence. As I shall argue below, however, we ought not to assume that a negative citation is indicative of a lack of influence.

[19] See further Arthur D. Austin, "Footnotes as Product Differentiation" (1987) 40 *Vanderbilt L. Rev.* 1131.

(principally academic) variant on power-dressing, whereby one uses citations, often voluminous citations, to create the impression of being thoroughly versed in the relevant literature.[20]

Note that as we expand this catalogue of reasons for engaging in citation, the reasons themselves are becoming increasingly less ingenuous. The activity of citing may sometimes be not so much the acknowledging of an influence or source as part of an effort to promote a particular strategy.[21] A citation can be a display of solidarity—an attempt to put a less senior colleague on the map, say, or a means of highlighting the initiatives of those with whom one shares an intellectual agenda.[22] It can also be an attempt at flattery—one might cite the works of those with whom one wants to curry favour (members of the editorial board of the journal to whom one is submitting one's article, for instance)[23]—or an effort to increase the number of citations to one's own works.[24] Citation can be interpreted as signalling behaviour: often we can get a fair idea of an author's perspective simply by looking at his or her citations, just as we might look at an academic journal and see from what is *not* being cited in the writings contained therein that it is unlikely to publish our work.[25] Citations may, furthermore, "signal to readers that the proffered article is the sort that they ought

[20] The context in which this particular phenomenon perhaps occurs most frequently is that of scholarship published in non-peer assessed American law school journals. See, e.g., J. M. Balkin and Sanford Levinson, "How to Win Cites and Influence People" (1996) 71 *Chicago-Kent L. Rev.* 843 at 960–1 (identifying and parodying the phenomenon). That "power-citation" tends to be fairly prevalent in these journals might be attributable to the fact that they are usually edited by students (who tend to make poor guardians against academic self-indulgence) and the fact that the task of footnoting is often completed, if not undertaken, by student-editors and research assistants.

[21] See generally Mengxiong Liu, "The Complexities of Citation Practice: A Review of Citation Studies" (1993) 49 *Jnl. of Documentation* 370.

[22] For illustrative discussions, see Harriet Zuckerman, "Citation Analysis and the Complex Problem of Intellectual Influence" (1987) 12 *Scientometrics* 329 at 332; Balkin and Levinson, *supra* n. 20, p.868; and Norman Kaplan, "The Norms of Citation Behaviour: Prolegomena to the Footnote" (1965) 16 *American Documentation* 179 at 181.

[23] See Dirk Schoonbaert and Gilbert Roelants, "Citation Analysis for Measuring the Value of Scientific Publications: Quality Assessment Tool or Comedy of Errors?" (1996) 1 *Tropical Medicine and International Health* 739 at 748.

[24] On reciprocality in citation, see Laura M. Baird and Charles Oppenheim, "Do Citations Matter?" (1994) 20 *Jnl. of Info. Science* 2 at 5; Michael E. Solimine, "The Impact of *Babcock* v. *Jackson*: An Empirical Note" (1993) 56 *Albany L. Rev.* 773 at 787–8; Jon Wiener, *Professors, Politics and Pop* (London, Verso, 1991), p.343; and Balkin and Levinson, *supra* n. 20, p.859.

[25] It is also possible, of course, for an author deliberately to cite materials which will make his or her work look attractive to a specific journal or publisher. See Baird and Oppenheim, *supra* n. 24, p.6.

to be interested in because it is based on the work of people they already know and trust"[26]—or the opposite.

It may also be the case that one cites certain works in order to be associated with greatness. One of Oliver Wendell Holmes's biographers has noted that writing about Holmes "can be likened to playing Hamlet in the theatre: it is a kind of apprenticeship that legal scholars undertake as a way of measuring their fitness to endure the academic travails ahead".[27] This likeness might be extended: writing about Holmes puts one in the company of the great. The citation of those of Holmes's stature, moreover, may send out a signal concerning one's intellectual aspirations and the company one wishes to keep. This strategy is slightly different from that of power-citing; for an author may cite sparingly but discriminately, creating the impression that he or she cares not for the thoughts of the *hoi polloi* but only for those of the grand masters.

Our general predilection for citing the great over and above the not-so-great is evidenced by what citation analysts have termed "the Matthew effect".[28] Academic esteem tends to cultivate itself: rewards tend to be skewed towards those who are already highly reputed.[29] Faced with the choice of attributing an idea to a renowned academic or to a relative unknown, our tendency is to regard citation of the former as the safest option, much as we might be inclined more generally to choose products which have recognized brand-names.[30] The principal explanation for this tendency is that the information costs of citing particular authors decrease as their citation counts increase. Citations may lead to a person becoming more widely known within their particular sphere. Where this happens, others within that sphere will have to invest less in finding out about that person's reputation as compared with the reputations of those who are less frequently cited.[31] Not only is there a greater likelihood that those intending to cite will find the relevant work of the more highly reputed person more easy to recall and

[26] Balkin and Levinson, *supra* n. 20, p.868.

[27] G. Edward White, *Intervention and Detachment: Essays in Legal History and Jurisprudence* (New York, Oxford University Press, 1994), p.75.

[28] See Matthew 13: 12 ("the man who has will be given more"); also Matthew 25: 29.

[29] "[T]he Matthew effect consists in the accruing of greater increments of recognition for particular scientific contributions to scientists of considerable repute and the withholding of such recognition from scientists who have not yet made their mark": Robert K. Merton, "The Matthew Effect in Science" (1968) n.s. 159 *Science* 56 at 58.

[30] See Sherwin Rosen, "The Economics of Superstars" (1981) 71 *Am. Econ. Rev*. 845.

[31] See Moshe Adler, "Stardom and Talent" (1985) 75 *Am. Econ. Rev*. 208.

locate, but citation to a renowned work may convey more information to readers than would be the case if a lesser-known work were cited.

The form of citation which will most often (though by no means always) be considered disingenuous is citation of oneself. Since this study, in so far as it focuses on citation, is concerned with the citation of the works of one group of people (academic lawyers) by another group (judges), the phenomenon of self-citation is not especially germane to our discussion. However, the phenomenon is not irrelevant to our analysis; for a primary motive for self-citation is to make one's opinions more visible to others. Self-citation might be regarded as, among other things, a form of advertising which aims to generate "sales" (i.e., citations).[32] One might question just how many of the motives for citing considered above can ever be relevant or identifiable in the context of judges citing scholars. Many reasons for citing derive their validity primarily from norms and strategies which operate predominantly within the academic system: while one academic may be motivated to cite another or others in order to highlight scholarly disagreement, differentiate product, display solidarity, flattery or apparent erudition, it is unlikely that judges will cite for such purposes. Although judges may quite often cite juristic commentary in order to disagree with it, judicial citations to scholarship generally seem bereft of academic agenda. This does not lead to the conclusion, however, that nearly all of the motives considered above are irrelevant to this study. For the successful pursuit of these motives by academics may have an impact on what the courts find useful. If courts (and, for that matter, counsel), in so far as they are concerned with scholarship, seek out the works of the most reputable academic lawyers, and if the reputations of academic lawyers are to some degree measured by citation frequency, then one's capacity successfully to pursue citation-enhancing strategies *might* increase the chances of one's scholarship influencing judges.

The critical question here—the question which we have delayed addressing—concerns the relationship between citation and influence. There are strong grounds for making a connection between citation and influence. Many citation analysts agree that it will be unlikely that a highly-cited document has not been influential in some way or

[32] See William M. Landes, Lawrence Lessig and Michael E. Solimine, "Judicial Influence: A Citation Analysis of Federal Courts of Appeals Judges" (1998) 27 *J. Leg. Studs.* 271 at 274.

another.[33] The fact that the work of Professor X is regularly cited by counsel and judges will most likely mean that his or her opinion generally counts among counsel and judges, for academic opinions which barristers and judges consider not to count will tend to be ignored. Research in certain disciplines has demonstrated positive correlations between the frequency with which a document is cited and the impact of that document within the relevant research environment.[34] It is worth noting also that citation counts have in the past proved reliable predictors as regards the recipients of prestigious academic honours.[35] To assert without qualification that "citations are measures of intellectual influence"[36] would be rash. But it would also be rash not to recognize that citation counts can be a valuable source of information when endeavouring to assess influence.[37] Even though analyses of citations cannot enable us to measure definitively the influence of a particular work, they can provide some impression of the extent to which that work has been influential.

Yet for all that the exercise of estimating influence by counting citations may be a valuable one, it needs to be undertaken with caution.

[33] See, e.g., Theodore Eisenberg and Martin T. Wells, "Ranking and Explaining the Scholarly Impact of Law Schools" (1998) 27 *J. Leg. Studs*. 373 at 377 ("Appearing on lists of the most-cited articles is rarely viewed as damning of one's work"); Schoonbaert and Roelants, *supra* n. 23, p.748; Coase, *supra* n. 18, pp.809–10; and Posner, *supra* n. 17, p.17.

[34] See, e.g., Julie Virgo, "A Statistical Procedure for Evaluating the Importance of Scientific Papers" (1977) 47 *Library Quarterly* 415; Henry Small, "A Co-citation Model of a Scientific Speciality: A Longitudinal Study of Collagen Research" (1977) 7 *Social Studies of Science* 139; and Michael E. D. Koenig, "A Bibliometric Analysis of Pharmaceutical Research" (1983) 12 *Research Policy* 15.

[35] It may well be, of course, that the correlation between frequent citation and the award of high academic honours is largely indicative of the ability of prize committees to be swayed by high citation counts. The studies evidencing the correlation tend, nevertheless, to offer some fairly striking figures. One study, for example, found that in 1961 the average physicist was cited 5.5 times, that those who received the Nobel prize between 1956 and 1960 were cited an average of 42 times, and that those who were to receive the prize between 1961 and 1965 were cited an average of 62 times: see Stephen Cole and Jonathan R. Cole, "Scientific Output and Recognition: A Study in the Operation of the Reward System in Science" (1967) 32 *Am. Sociol. Rev*. 377. See also Susan V. Ashton and C. Oppenheim, "A Method of Predicting Nobel Prizewinners in Chemistry" (1978) 8 *Social Studies of Science* 341; and Eugene Garfield, "Do Nobel Prize Winners Write Citation Classics?" (1986) 23 *Current Contents* 3.

[36] George J. Stigler, *The Economist as Preacher and Other Essays* (Chicago, University of Chicago Press, 1982), p.173. Although Stigler opens his chapter on the pattern of citation practices in economics with this statement, his discussion of citations is nuanced and does not straightforwardly equate citation frequency with influence.

[37] See Eugene Garfield, "From Citation Indexes to Informetrics: Is the Tail Now Wagging the Dog?" (1998) 48 *Libri* 67 at 78.

Citation is not necessarily indicative of influence.[38] As has been noted already, citations to a document may accrue owing to the operation of dynamics—such as the Matthew effect—which cannot satisfactorily be explained in terms of influence. A document might be cited regularly, moreover, not because it is influential but because it is a good or convenient source of information or because it summarizes a particular idea or issue effectively.[39] To be popular is not necessarily to be influential, and to be influential is not necessarily to be popular. Documents might sometimes be cited almost reflexively because they have acquired an iconic status; many of the citations to those documents will mirror not so much what the documents say as what they have come to represent. Since some such documents will represent more or less all things to all people—literary Rorschach tests—they will be especially amenable to citation.[40]

Just as citations do not necessarily indicate influence, degrees of influence will not always be captured by citation. Possibly I am mistaken in my belief that there is one legal philosopher who has especially influenced my approach to jurisprudence; all I am certain of is that I rarely cite him. At a more general level, although counting citations to the works of, say, Charles Darwin or Karl Marx will no doubt indicate that these writers have been influential, it seems unlikely that such counting could ever do justice to the nature and extent of their impact on social thought.[41] A citation to a modern work might conceal the original source of influence. "Any article in modern economics which cited its direct sources would perhaps name modern articles and

[38] See generally Zuckerman, *supra* n. 22, *passim*.

[39] See, e.g., Marc Galanter, "This Week's Citation Classic" (1983) 5 *Current Contents* 24, discussing how his frequently-cited article, "Why the 'Haves' Come Out Ahead: Speculations on the Limits of Legal Change" (1974) 9 *Law & Society Rev.* 95, is "often cited to acknowledge the terms 'repeat player' and (less often) 'one shotter' that have been widely used to refer to recurrent and occasional users of legal process". This should not, of course, be taken to suggest that Galanter's article has been only superficially influential.

[40] For illustrative discussions, see Richard L. Marcus, "*Public Law Litigation* and Legal Scholarship" (1988) 21 *Univ. Michigan Jnl. of Law Reform* 647 at 655–6; Balkin and Levinson, *supra* n. 20, pp.861–4.

[41] With regard to Karl Marx, it is interesting to note one particular observation offered by Snyder in his study of citations to great authors by the United States Supreme Court throughout the period 1790–1986. According to Snyder, references to Marx by Supreme Court Justices are often misleading because he is rarely being cited for his wisdom. "More often, his name appears in cases where his followers are being prosecuted": Fritz Snyder, "The Great Authors and Their Influence on the Supreme Court" (1987) 7 *Legal Reference Services Quarterly* 285 at 287.

books", it has been claimed, "but they would soon be traced back to [Alfred] Marshall, and then to earlier writers".[42] When the influence of a work becomes particularly profound, citations to it may decrease: the phenomenon of eponymic citation—those instances in which an idea becomes associated with a name (Pareto optimality, Occam's razor, the Coase theorem and so on)—indicates as much. Indeed, although a substantial number of works are cited rarely because they are uninfluential, a much smaller number are cited rarely because they have been extremely influential. Einstein's paper on the special theory of relativity is a case in point: while his theory and his equation of $E = mc^2$ have been profoundly influential within modern science, the paper in which he expounded the theory and formulated the equation is, as compared with many more modern papers on relativity, cited infrequently.[43] The ideas of the greatest innovators are often considered not to require explicit citation because they have become embedded in our intellectual culture.

Although analyses of citations can reveal influence, they may also generate distortions. We have observed already that not all citations are of the same type. It is tempting to move from this observation to the claim that distorted estimations of influence will be produced where citation analyses fail to distinguish between those references which are critical and those which are favourable. This move entails, however, the assumption that the critical citation must be less demonstrative of influence than the favourable citation. We might question whether, in general, this assumption holds good. Those works which fail to make an impact on us we tend to ignore rather than to criticize; and so the fact that we have bothered to cite critically might reasonably be taken as a gauge of influence. (Indeed, we might speculate that whereas many favourable citations will in fact be efforts to flatter others, display

[42] Stigler, *supra* n. 36, p.184. It is worth noting also that recent works might sometimes be cited in preference to older ones not because they are better or more apt, but because they are physically or terminologically more accessible or because they provide a medium through which to praise or attack one's contemporaries. See Richard A. Posner, *Cardozo: A Study in Reputation* (Chicago, University of Chicago Press, 1990), pp.70–1.

[43] See Eugene Garfield, *Essays of an Information Scientist: Volume Five (1981–1982)* (Philadelphia, ISI Press, 1983), pp.91–5. For the original paper, see Albert Einstein, "Zur Elektrodynamik bewegter Körper [On the Electrodynamics of Moving Bodies]" (1905) 17 *Ann. Phys. Leipzig* 891. Garfield's citation analysis of this paper includes references to reprints and translations.

solidarity or increase one's cachet, critical citations are more likely to be "sincere" and therefore more accurate indicators of influence.)[44]

The distortions which citation analyses can produce tend to arise out of methodology. Counting citations to a single work, for example, might create an inaccurate impression of the influence of its author. An academic might produce works nearly all of which attract healthy, albeit not especially high, numbers of citations; to count the citations to any one of that person's works will suggest that he or she is only moderately influential. Were we to consider citations to that person's work *en masse*, however, we would probably reach a different conclusion.[45] When analysing citations for the purpose of assessing influence, it may also be important to consider who is doing the citing: scholarship which is regularly cited by academics might not strike a chord with judges,[46] just as works of academics which meet with widespread judicial approval might be largely overlooked by other scholars.[47] Estimations of the influence of particular documents by reference to the extent to which they have been cited may require, furthermore, that one takes account of just how long the documents have been in the public domain. The longer the period of time since the publication of an article, the more citations that article will accrue. If article A (published four years ago) has, at this point in time, received eighty citations and article B (published twelve years ago) has received 240 citations, we might expect, *ceteris paribus*, that the two articles will, judged in terms of citation-counts, prove over time to be more or less equally influential. At this specific point in time, however, the counting of citations creates the impression that B must be considerably more influential than A. It may well be, of course, that B is more influential than A—this will most likely be the case, for example, if citations to A have more or less peaked (making it unlikely that A will receive 160 or more cita-

[44] One commentator has argued that a work of legal scholarship will sometimes be cited "because it constitutes 'the classic mistake': some work is so wrong, or so bad, that everyone acknowledges it for that reason". Brian Leiter, "Measuring the Academic Distinction of Law Faculties" (2000) 29 *J. Leg. Studs*. 451 at 469–70. The case of Langdellian formalism seems to support this point. Interestingly, while Langdell and his cohort are commonly cited critically by American academic lawyers, it is difficult to imagine any American lawyer concluding that Landgellianism has not been influential.

[45] For illustration, see William M. Landes and Richard A. Posner, "Heavily Cited Articles in Law" (1996) 71 *Chicago-Kent L. Rev*. 825 at 827.

[46] See Marcus, *supra* n. 40, *passim*.

[47] See Balkin and Levinson, *supra* n. 20, pp.865–6; Posner, *supra* n. 42, p.79.

tions in the next eight years).[48] This qualification does not detract from, but rather reinforces, the central point: that citation analyses may generate misleading impressions of influence if they take no account of longevity.[49]

The argument advanced in this section might be summarized thus: analyses of citations may prove helpful for the purpose of assessing influence, but they must always be treated with circumspection. We will see later in this study that citation analysis is sometimes unhelpful for the purpose of assessing the influence of scholarship on courts because the citations are simply not there to be analysed. We will also see that non-citation does not necessarily indicate absence of influence. If this is so, one might ask, should we not view with total scepticism any effort to assess influence by reference to citations? The reason that we ought not to be so sceptical is that citations sometimes do reflect influence: we shall see as much in the next chapter (though we will also see there that rarely is the connection between citation and influence easily made). For the remainder of this chapter, we will move away from the idea that influence might be measured by the analysis of citations and consider instead the factors which make influence difficult not only to measure but also to identify.

THE ELUSIVENESS OF INFLUENCE

Can academics do anything to ensure that their works will influence judges? While there are things that they can do which will increase their prospects of being influential, there appear to be no strategies which guarantee success. Most legal scholarship, whether considered in relation to courts or any other group of people, is markedly uninfluential.[50]

[48] If A were a law review article, the likelihood is that citations to it would have peaked: see Ian Ayres and Fredrick E. Vars, "Determinants of Citations to Articles in Elite Law Reviews" (2000) 29 *J. Leg. Studs.* 427 at 436 (showing that citations to American law review articles tend to peak four years after publication). On citation life-cycles in other disciplines, see V. Cano and N. C. Lind, "Citation Life-Cycles of Ten Citation Classics" (1991) 22 *Scientometrics* 297 (examining citation rates in medicine and biochemistry).

[49] On the significance of age, both of work and of producers of work, for the purpose of explaining scholarly citations, see William M. Landes and Richard A. Posner, "Citations, Age, Fame, and the Web" (2000) 29 *J. Leg. Studs.* 319 at 321–9.

[50] See Richard A. Posner, *Overcoming Law* (Cambridge, Mass., Harvard University Press, 1995), pp.99–100 (developing the argument that "[s]cholarship, like salmon breeding in the wild, is a high-risk, low-return activity").

Those who do produce influential work may find its influence to be short-lived.[51] In so far as scholarship can be of influence, moreover, the odds of producing influential work are—this is the so-called Matthew effect—stacked in favour of those who already enjoy academic renown.

Even the most highly reputed scholars may struggle to orchestrate influence. Indeed, few academics who set out to produce scholarship which will influence judges are likely to be successful. A comparison might be drawn here with the phenomenon of regulatory failure: just as regulatory initiatives can sometimes prove ineffectual or even counter-productive, so too efforts to be influential can prove fruitless or have unintended consequences.[52] There are, of course, strategies and mechanisms which may enhance one's profile, various forms of networking, enlightened career moves, the Matthew effect, the successful adoption of citation-enhancing strategies and so on. But while such strategies and mechanisms may increase one's general chances of being an influential scholar, they are unlikely to ensure that any specific piece of work which one produces will influence others.

Sometimes, the influence of an academic's work appears at least in part to derive from his or her indifference to influence. Although Ronald Coase, for example, has clearly intended to contribute to economic thought, he has always purported to be detached from the concerns of academic lawyers.[53] Yet citations to his writings suggest that his influence on modern American legal scholarship has been profound.[54] No doubt numerous reasons explain Coase's influence within the field of law, not least the fact that his work raises interesting (and troubling) questions for lawyers. There is also the fact that, having been lauded by American academic lawyers, he has generally failed to return the compliment: while his work may fascinate them, their work

[51] Perhaps this is less so in law as compared with some other disciplines: see Balkin and Levinson, *supra* n. 20, p.851; and cf. Stigler, *supra* n. 36, pp.181–2.

[52] See Gerald L. Neuman, "Law Review Articles that Backfire" (1988) 21 *Univ. Mich. J. Law Reform* 697.

[53] "I have no interest in lawyers or legal education . . . My interest is in economics, and I was interested in carrying forward the *Journal of Law & Economics* because I thought it would change what economists did": comments attributed to Ronald Coase in Edmund W. Kitch (ed.), "The Fire of Truth: A Remembrance of Law and Economics at Chicago, 1932–1970" (1983) 26 *J. Law & Econ.* 163 at 192. See also Coase, *supra* n. 18, p.809 ("It was no part of my intention to contribute to legal scholarship").

[54] See, e.g., Landes and Posner, *supra* n. 1, p.405; Shapiro, "The Most-Cited Law Review Articles Revisited", *supra* n. 14, p.759.

does not really intrigue him.[55] This last observation perhaps puts one in mind of (though it is not quite the same as) Groucho Marx's famous quip that he would not dream of belonging to a club that was willing to have him as a member. In a world in which a premium is placed on discovering and adopting strategies for making a positive impact on one's peers, the person who exhibits no intention to make an impression on others—who is not so much disdainful of the club as simply uninterested in it—is perhaps likely, if not to impress others, at least to seem enigmatic and possibly charismatic to them. Strategies aimed at getting other people to be impressed with one's work or behaviour are often self-defeating.[56] In contexts where people generally invest heavily in such strategies, there may be a tendency to respect insouciance.

Not only does influence resist precise measurement, then, but—when considered in the context of scholarship and its relationship to judicial thought—it is likely to be impervious to orchestration. It seems that everything that might be said about influence testifies to its elusiveness. Other than citations, what other possible indicators of influence might be identified? It is important to confront this question, for in some jurisdictions courts have traditionally been reluctant to cite scholarly works. If citation is the only meaningful indicator that we have, the effort to identify whether academics have had any influence on courts will, with respect to certain judicial cultures, prove doomed. But what else *do* we have?

Citations seem generally to be the most reliable and identifiable indicators of influence. But they are not the only indicators. There are other factors on which the student of influence might usefully focus. It is often important, for example, to try to assess the personal qualities of those whom one suspects of having been influential. Benjamin Cardozo's influence as a judge, for example, was to a significant degree attributable to his admirable human qualities.[57] We will see in Chapter 5 that both Frederick Pollock and Arthur Goodhart, as editors of the *Law Quarterly Review*, were to a certain degree able to influence English judges through the pages of that journal. Evidence of this

[55] See further Neil Duxbury, "Ronald's Way", in S. G. Medema (ed.), *Coasean Economics: Law and Economics and the New Institutional Economics* (Boston, Kluwer, 1998), pp.185–92.

[56] See Jon Elster, *Sour Grapes: Studies in the Subversion of Rationality* (Cambridge, Cambridge University Press, 1983), pp.66–71; also Harold Bloom, *The Anxiety of Influence: A Theory of Poetry* (New York, Oxford University Press, 1973), p.11 (on the idea that "influence cannot be willed").

[57] See Posner, *supra* n. 42, pp.130–2.

influence comes, in the main, not from judicial citations of their writings but from anecdotes concerning their roles as informal judicial advisors. Qualities such as integrity, energy, perspicacity, diplomacy, entrepreneurship, candour, charisma, intellectual prestige and renown may translate into influence.[58] Besides seeking out—and especially in the absence of—citations to a person's work, we may do well to try to locate accounts of his or her qualities. Such accounts might at least provide clues concerning the influence of that person's work.

Efforts to estimate influence require sensitivity to the peculiarities of different legal cultures. We will see in the next chapter that citation analysis is well suited to the study of the influence of scholarship on the courts in the USA. But it is not as well suited to such study in relation to either France or England. Within different cultures, moreover, specific conventions and traditions might affect the extent to which scholarship impacts upon the judicial process. It is well known, for example, that many American judges delegate to their clerks much of the responsibility for researching, and even writing, opinions.[59] Research suggests that legal scholarship sometimes acquires significance in the context of American judicial decisions owing to the fact that law clerks, in their memoranda and opinion drafts, often have a

[58] For a study of how prestige can translate into influence, for example, see David Klein and Darby Morrisroe, "The Prestige and Influence of Individual Judges on the U. S. Courts of Appeals" (1999) 28 *J. Leg. Studs*. 371. The translation of entrepreneurship into influence is particularly well illustrated by the career of the neo-classical law and economics votary, Henry G. Manne: see *Symposium: The Legacy of Henry G. Manne—Pioneer in Law & Economics and Innovator in Legal Education* (1999) 50 *Case Western Reserve L. Rev*. 203, and especially the articles by Ronald A. Cass (pp.203–14), George L. Priest (pp.325–31), Paul H. Rubin (pp.333–50), Henry N. Butler (pp.351–420) and Jack B. Weinstein (pp.421–9).

[59] See Richard A. Posner, *The Federal Courts: Challenge and Reform* (Cambridge, Mass., Harvard University Press, 1996), pp.139–59. Another Federal appellate judge remarks that she and her peers "write 40–80 law-making opinions each year . . . Those opinions contain myriad case citations; except for those of a handful of purist holdouts, they are generously footnoted. A judge simply can't do all that by herself. A few try . . . but they become rarer as time goes by. Actually, even when I clerked for an illustrious pathbreaking judge back in the early 1950s, I wrote many of his first drafts. I suspect the practice goes back even further": Patricia M. Wald, "How I Write" (1993) 4 *Scribes Jnl. of Legal Writing* 55 at 59. Wald's suspicion that the practice was accepted before the 1950s seems well-founded. Dean Acheson, who served as a law clerk under Justice Louis Brandeis, remarked apropos of the latter's opinion in *Ruppert* v. *Caffey*, 251 U. S. 264 (1920) that although Brandeis wrote the opinion, he wrote the footnotes: Dean Acheson, "Recollections of Service with the Federal Supreme Court" (1957) 17 *Alabama Lawyer* 355, cited after Chester A. Newland, "Innovation in Judicial Technique: The Brandeis Opinion" (mimeograph, Idaho State College, Government Faculty Seminar, Pocatello, Idaho, 9 February 1960), p.13.

tendency to cite academic writings (very often the writings of those who taught them).[60] More generally, the influence of academic writings within any legal system will to a large extent be dependent on the historical relationship between jurist and judge. In attempting to assess the influence of scholarship on the courts within any jurisdiction, it is important to take account of the extent to which judges have traditionally been willing to consider the views of academic lawyers. In those systems where judges have traditionally given jurists the cold shoulder, the chances are that old habits will die hard even if some of the modern members of the judiciary are receptive to scholarly opinion.

We should also note, before concluding, that the extent to which legal scholarship is likely to come to the attention of judges will vary from one jurisdiction to the next. To publish is to advertise one's scholarly wares; within the academic realm as elsewhere, however, some forms of advertisement tend to be more successful than others. We will see in Chapter 4 that, in France, case notes are published not in academic law journals but in case reports, underneath the relevant decisions. Within the French legal tradition, the case note tends to be not only a commentary but also—owing to the fact that the *rapport* of the reporter judge and the *conclusions* of the *ministère public* are rarely published—a valuable source of information. In short, French case notes are highly visible and, so far as practitioners and judges are concerned, often indispensable. In England, case notes do not command quite the same degree of respect as they do in France. One of the reasons for this is perhaps that English case notes are usually (though not always) published in journals devoted exclusively to academic commentary. Indeed it is mainly in those areas of English law where case notes and case reports do often appear side-by-side, areas such as family law, planning law and criminal law, that the influence of academic case commentary on judicial thought is particularly evident.

In this chapter, I have attempted to outline the ways in which we might identify and assess the influence of scholarship on courts. I have

[60] See Louis J. Sirico and Jeffrey B. Margulies, "The Citing of Law Reviews by the Supreme Court: An Empirical Study" (1986) 34 *U.C.L.A. L. Rev.* 131 at 133–4. The tendency of many law clerks to cite legal scholarship might be largely attributable to the fact that most of them are recent law graduates, and also to the fact that many of them are of an academic bent—indeed, a significant proportion of those who complete judicial clerkships proceed to become law professors: see Robert J. Borthwick and Jordan R. Schau, "Gatekeepers of the Profession: An Empirical Profile of the Nation's Law Professors" (1991) 25 *Univ. Michigan J. Law Reform* 191 at 214–17.

also tried to emphasize the nebulous nature of influence, and to draw attention to the fact that grappling with the concept can prove hazardous. Citations, usually the best proxy for influence, can be accompanied by various forms of distortion and do not always translate into the real thing. In so far as influences are traceable at all, they will often have their roots in more than one source. Those sources of influence might not have immediate effects: over a lengthy period of time, a body of academic work might have a cumulative impact on judicial thought; or the influence of a single piece of work might only very gradually become apparent.[61] Judges, in so far as they are concerned with scholarship, will most likely lack both the time and the inclination to scrutinize developments in the literature with the same degree of enthusiasm as most academic specialists.[62] It may well be, over time, that scholarly influence creeps up on the courts, that the significance of a certain piece or body of scholarship gradually gains judicial recognition. But this process of osmosis might not be reflected by citations in judicial opinions. It may be the case, moreover, that when judges do cite academic works, they sometimes cite not those which have influenced their thought over an extended period of time but only those which reflect their views as of now.[63]

In what follows, we will have the opportunity to glimpse many of the various dynamics of influence at work. Different dynamics are more or less prominent from one jurisdiction to the next (which explains why there exists the problem of incommensurability to which we referred in the Introduction). We turn next to the USA, where judges have for many decades demonstrated a willingness to cite legal scholarship in their opinions. This willingness is generally taken to indicate that American judges are by and large receptive to the ideas and arguments of academic lawyers. As a general assumption, this seems sound. The basic purpose of the next chapter, none the less, is to try to show that as regards the relationship between academic lawyers and judges, matters in the USA are not quite so clear-cut as they might at first appear. Academic writings influence judges, but this influence looks different under close scrutiny than it perhaps does to many casual observers.

[61] See John Gava, "Scholarship and Community" (1994) 16 *Sydney L. Rev.* 443 at 449.

[62] See Meir Dan-Cohen, "Listeners and Eavesdroppers: Substantive Legal Theory and Its Audience" (1992) 63 *Univ. Colorado L. Rev.* 569.

[63] See Edward L. Rubin, "What Does Prescriptive Legal Scholarship Say and Who is Listening to It: A Response to Professor Dan-Cohen" (1992) 63 *Univ. Colorado L. Rev.* 731 at 750.

3

The USA

FOR MANY a legal scholar located elsewhere, the American law school looks like the land of plenty. Research support in the forms of funding and student assistance is rarely in short supply. Even at the less renowned law schools, the libraries tend to be well-stocked and the computer facilities state-of-the-art. Since almost every American law faculty boasts at least one (normally student-edited) law journal, the fear of being unable to find a publisher seems not to exist.[1] In academic life as elsewhere, one looks to the USA to find lower prices and larger sizes: American law books and journals are, by British standards, generally cheap and the law reviews regularly publish articles four times the length of the average British law journal essay. From an outsider's perspective, there is much about the American academic-legal scene that looks enviable.

Yet in every dream-home we may find heartache. Even American legal academics sometimes question whether their riches bring out the best in them. By the end of the twentieth century, legal scholarship in some of the most highly reputed American law journals was being condemned as self-indulgent, verbose, abstruse, excessively footnoted, unconstructive, methodologically jejune, jargon-laden and—as regards the concerns of practising lawyers—irrelevant. More often than not, the condemnations were being levelled by legal scholars themselves.[2]

[1] Traditionally, the student-edited law school review has been the primary forum for the publication of legal scholarship in the USA. Besides being responsible for editing the articles which appear in the law school reviews, students are also responsible for producing many of the notes and case commentaries published therein. (Case note writing, with which we will be concerned in the next two chapters, is an activity which—should they engage in it at all—American academics tend to consign to their student days.)

[2] See, e.g., Kenneth Lasson, "Scholarship Amok: Excesses in the Pursuit of Truth and Tenure" (1990) 103 *Harv. L. Rev.* 926; Pierre Schlag, *Laying Down the Law: Mysticism, Fetishism, and the American Legal Mind* (New York, New York University Press, 1996), pp.17–41; Richard Delgado, "Norms and Normal Science: Toward a Critique of Normativity in Legal Thought" (1991) 139 *Univ. Pennsylvania L. Rev.* 933; Paul D. Carrington, "Butterfly Effects: The Possibilities of Law Teaching in a Democracy" (1992) 41 *Duke L. J.* 741 at 800–3; David P. Bryden, "Scholarship about Scholarship" (1992) 63 *Univ. Colorado L. Rev.* 641; Steven Lubet, "Is Legal Theory Good for Anything?" [1997] *Univ. Illinois L. Rev.* 193; Alex M. Johnson, Jr., "Think Like a Lawyer, Work Like a

Throughout the twentieth century, the relationship between the courts and the law schools in the USA was generally a healthy one. Academics tried to influence judicial thought, and judges by and large appreciated (or certainly were not offended by) their efforts. By the end of the century, however, the relationship had been thrown into question. Not only had certain law professors become sceptical about the capacity for scholarship to influence the work of the courts, but in the courts themselves there had evolved some dismay concerning the apparent indifference of many legal academics towards the concerns and expectations of the judiciary. In the early 1990s, a prominent American circuit judge (and former academic) argued that too many law professors were disregarding the relationship that they had traditionally enjoyed with the judiciary: although these academics were in a position to be able to influence judges and other members of the legal profession—so the argument went—a significant number of them showed no desire to be so influential.[3] In England, as we will see in Chapter 5, the relationship between judges and academic lawyers might be presented as a story about clouds with silver linings. In the USA, the relationship can be characterized as the story of a sunny day which turns hazy.

JUDGES ON SCHOLARSHIP

Citation of legal periodical literature in Supreme Court opinions can be traced back to at least 1900.[4] Since American judges never adopted the English convention against the citation of the works of living commentators as authority, it is perhaps not surprising to find that twentieth-century American legal literature offers plenty of judicial tributes to legal scholarship.[5] "More and more we are looking to the scholar in his

Machine: The Dissonance Between Law School and Law Practice" (1991) 64 *Southern Calif. L. Rev.* 1231.

[3] Harry T. Edwards, "The Growing Disjunction Between Legal Education and the Legal Profession" (1992) 91 *Michigan L. Rev.* 34.

[4] See Wes Daniels, "'Far Beyond the Law Reports': Secondary Source Citations in United States Supreme Court Opinions October Terms 1900, 1940, and 1978" (1983) 76 *Law Library Jnl.* 1 at 15.

[5] On the American avoidance of the "better read when dead" convention, see Borris M. Komar, "Text-Books As Authority in Anglo-American Law" (1923) 11 *Calif. L. Rev.* 397 at 408–9; Borris M. Komar, "Probative Force of Authoritative Law-Works: Works on the Law-Merchant" (1924) 4 *Boston Univ. L. Rev.* 191 at 193; and Max Radin, "Sources of Law—New and Old" (1928) 1 *Southern Calif. L. Rev.* 411 at 415.

study, to the jurist rather than to the judge or lawyer, for inspiration and guidance", Benjamin Cardozo wrote in 1923.[6] "[L]eadership in the march of legal thought", he observed only a few years later, "has been passing in our day from the benches of the courts to the chairs of universities"; and "[t]his change of leadership has stimulated a willingness to cite the law review essays in briefs and in opinions in order to buttress a conclusion".[7]

In his 1923 lectures, Cardozo pointed to a decision of his own court, the New York Court of Appeals, to illustrate how law review articles could influence judicial thought.[8] The illustration was by no means an isolated one. One of the earliest articles to appear in the *Harvard Law Review*, Warren and Brandeis's "The Right to Privacy",[9] is often lauded as an "outstanding example of the influence of legal periodicals upon the American law".[10] Brandeis in particular was a keen advocate of the law reviews—he had helped to establish the *Harvard Law Review*[11]—and was eager, in his capacity as a Justice of the United States Supreme Court, to see his brethren resort to them in order to ascertain factual data and discover academic opinions on doctrinal

[6] Benjamin N. Cardozo, *The Growth of the Law* (Westport, Conn., Greenwood Press, 1973 [1924]), p.11. This book comprises a series of lectures which Cardozo presented at the Yale Law School in December 1923.

[7] Benjamin N. Cardozo, "Introduction", in G. J. Thompson *et al.* (eds), *Selected Readings on the Law of Contracts from American and English Periodicals* (New York, Macmillan, 1931), pp.vii–xi at ix.

[8] See Cardozo, *supra* n. 6, pp.13–16. Cardozo was elected to the New York Court of Appeals in 1917 and became Chief Judge of the Court in 1927. In 1932, he was appointed by President Herbert Hoover to the United States Supreme Court. See generally Andrew L. Kaufman, *Cardozo* (Cambridge, Mass., Harvard University Press, 1998), pp.162–96.

[9] Samuel D. Warren and Louis D. Brandeis, "The Right to Privacy" (1890) 4 *Harv. L. Rev.* 193. While it is important to take account of this article for the purpose of registering the influence of law review writing on American judicial thought, its relevance to this particular study is in fact somewhat limited—for although Warren and Brandeis were writing for a law review, they were practising rather than academic lawyers.

[10] William L. Prosser, "Privacy" (1960) 48 *Calif. L. Rev.* 383. For illustrations of its influence on judicial thought, see Note, "The Right to Privacy" (1891) 5 *Harv. L. Rev.* 148; and Denis O'Brien, "The Right of Privacy" (1902) 2 *Columb. L. Rev.* 438. For discussions of its influence more generally, see Palmer D. Edmunds, "Hail to Law Reviews" (1967) 1 *John Marshall Jnl. of Practice and Procedure* 1 at 2–4; James H. Barron, "Warren and Brandeis, *The Right to Privacy*, 4 Harv. L. Rev. 193 (1890): Demystifying a Landmark Citation" (1979) 13 *Suffolk University L. Rev.* 875; Michael J. Swygert and Jon W. Bruce, "The Historical Origins, Founding, and Early Development of Student-Edited Law Reviews" (1985) 36 *Hastings L. J.* 739 at 787–8; and Mary Ann Glendon, *Rights Talk: The Impoverishment of Political Discourse* (New York, Free Press, 1991), pp.54–5.

[11] See Philippa Strum, *Louis D. Brandeis: Justice for the People* (Cambridge, Mass., Harvard University Press, 1984), p.363.

issues. In his dissent in *Adams* v. *Tanner*, handed down in 1917, Brandeis cited numerous academic (and other) writings in explaining the state regulation of employment agencies and the policy considerations behind Washington's restriction on private employment offices.[12] In *Erie Railroad Co.* v. *Tompkins* (1938), he referred to no fewer than twenty-eight works of scholarship.[13] By the time of his retirement, Brandeis had written forty-seven opinions—twenty-five Court opinions, twenty dissents and two concurrences—in which he had cited law review articles.[14]

Not only was Brandeis willing to be influenced by, but he also wished to be an influence on, the law reviews. Regularly he would write to Felix Frankfurter with suggestions for topics and judicial decisions that merited coverage in the *Harvard Law Review*.[15] "Brandeis bombarded Frankfurter with ideas for articles on diversity of citizenship jurisdiction and on what he considered to be the misuse by the [Supreme] Court of the idea of a federal common law; then, when [in *Erie* v. *Tompkins*] Brandeis persuaded the Court to let him announce that there was no such thing as federal common law, his opinion cited one of the Frankfurter articles on the subject".[16] Levy and Murphy elaborate on this last point: "Brandeis had influenced the content of articles in the law journals to support a law which he and Frankfurter supported, and then used those articles [in *Erie*] to help persuade his

[12] *Adams* v. *Tanner* 244 U.S. 590, 597, 603 n. 3, 613 n. 1–3, 615 n. 1 (1917) (dissenting). In this case, the Supreme Court held that a Washington statute prohibiting employment agencies from receiving fees from workers for whom they found jobs was in violation of the Fourteenth Amendment.

[13] *Erie Railroad Co.* v. *Tomkins* 304 U.S. 64, 72 n. 3, 4, 73 n. 5, 6, 74 n. 7, 75 n. 9, 10, 77 n. 20–2 (1938).

[14] See John William Johnson, *The Dimensions of Non-Legal Evidence in the American Judicial Process: The Supreme Court's Use of Extra-Legal Materials in the Twentieth Century* (Ph.D. thesis, Graduate School, University of Minnesota, March 1974), p.133; and Chester A. Newland, "Innovation in Judicial Technique: The Brandeis Opinion" (mimeograph, Idaho State College, Government Faculty Seminar, Pocatello, Idaho, 9 February 1960), p.4.

[15] See David W. Levy and Bruce Allen Murphy, "Preserving the Progressive Spirit in a Conservative Time: The Joint Reform Efforts of Justice Brandeis and Professor Frankfurter, 1916–1933" (1980) 78 *Michigan L. Rev.* 1252 at 1285–91; and Bruce Allen Murphy, *The Brandeis/Frankfurter Connection: The Secret Political Activities of Two Supreme Court Justices* (New York, Oxford University Press, 1982), pp.73–97; though cf. Leonard Baker, *Brandeis and Frankfurter: A Dual Biography* (New York, Harper & Row, 1984), pp.240–1. On Frankfurter and Harvard, see H. N. Hirsch, *The Enigma of Felix Frankfurter* (New York, Basic Books, 1981), pp.20–5, 66–7; and for an interesting study of how Frankfurter himself influenced American legal thought, see Michael Ariens, "A Thrice-told Tale, Or Felix the Cat" (1994) 107 *Harv. L. Rev.* 620.

[16] Strum, *supra* n. 11, p.364.

colleagues on the Court to overturn the disfavored common-law rule".[17] It was noted in Chapter 2 that a person may sometimes cite others in an effort to raise the profile of his or her own works. Brandeis appears consciously to have adopted this strategy. Whether or not this be the case, it is clear that his acknowledgements of the initiatives of academics did not go unnoticed by academics themselves. He flattered them, and they returned the compliment: on his seventy-fifth birthday, three of the most prestigious law school journals dedicated issues to Brandeis and his jurisprudence.[18]

Perhaps no other early-twentieth century judge promoted the cause of the law review with Brandeis's passion and energy. Some judges were nevertheless keen, like Cardozo, to acknowledge the interplay between jurist and judge. In a paper delivered to the Association of American Law Schools in 1925, Learned Hand considered not what academics have to offer to judges, but what judges can teach academics. "[W]e are laborers in the same vineyard",[19] Hand noted:

> "[t]o you" [the legal scholar] I will ascribe the . . . function of systematizing, of rectifying and of clarifying what exists so that we [judges] shall know our possessions and be able to use our tools. To you too I will ascribe the still more excellent function of contriving new methods, of discovering new ideas, of surveying new territory, though in this we may at times have a not insignificant part. And to ourselves I reserve a more humble role; we are the mass from whom proceeds moral authority over the people. We furnish the momentum, you the direction; but each is necessary to the other, each must understand, respect and regard the other, or both will fail."[20]

There features in this passage a theme—judicial attestation to the importance of academic commentary—which recurs regularly throughout twentieth-century American legal writing. "[T]he articles contributed to the reviews by eminent legal experts have given lawyers and judges the benefit of wide research and exploration", the Chief Justice of the Supreme Court observed in 1941, "not infrequently blazing new trails in preference to old but less desirable paths".[21] "I have a

[17] Levy and Murphy, *supra* n. 15, p.1291.

[18] See (1931) 45 *Harv. L. Rev.* 1; (1931) 31 *Columbia L. Rev.* 1071; (1931) 41 *Yale L. J.* 1; and also Brandeis to Frankfurter, 19 November 1931, in M. I. Urofsky and D. W. Levy (eds), *"Half Brother, Half Son": The Letters of Louis D. Brandeis to Felix Frankfurter* (Norman, Okla., University of Oklahoma Press, 1991), p.471.

[19] Learned Hand, "Have the Bench and Bar Anything to Contribute to the Teaching of Law?" (1926) 24 *Michigan L. Rev.* 466.

[20] *Ibid.*, p.480.

[21] Charles E. Hughes, "Foreword" (1941) 50 *Yale L. J.* 737.

special affection for law reviews", wrote William O. Douglas in 1965, "and I have drawn heavily from them for ideas and guidance as practitioner, as teacher, and as judge".[22] Speaking in 1953 at a conference dedicated to law reviews, Judge Stanley Fuld proclaimed that judges "admire the law review for its scholarship, its accuracy, and, above all, for its excruciating fairness. We are well aware that the review takes very seriously its role as judge of judges—and to that, we say, more power to you".[23] For Chief Justice Warren, writing on the inauguration of the *UCLA Law Review* in 1953, "[t]he American law review properly has been called the most remarkable institution of the law school world . . . To a judge . . . the review may be both a severe critic and a helpful guide".[24] Three years later, on the anniversary of another review, he wrote of how "law reviews . . . help make the future path of the law".[25] Returning to the subject again in 1963, he claimed that "the law reviews . . . cannot do other than raise the standards of justice throughout the land".[26] "I salute them", one eminent Justice of the California Supreme Court (and former law professor) announced in 1962, "as the best critics a judge could have".[27] According to another member of that court, "[t]he relationship between the courts and law reviews resembles a long and happy marriage, and we in the judiciary are deeply grateful for our academic partners in our joint, never-ending quest for the just resolution of societal disputes".[28] In lauding the law reviews, American judges often pay tribute to the student editors and note-writers as well as to the academic contributors. "[T]he student writers . . . have themselves offered much that is constructive. Perhaps our sharpest critics, their disinterested inquiry is needed and appreciated".[29] "[W]hen I find that any opinion of mine has been approved by these young critics", the Chief Judge of the New York Court of

[22] William O. Douglas, "Law Reviews and Full Disclosure" (1965) 40 *Washington L. Rev.* 227.

[23] Stanley H. Fuld, "A Judge Looks at the Law Review" (1953) 28 *New York Univ. L. Rev.* 915 at 918.

[24] Earl Warren, "Messages of Greeting to the U.C.L.A. Law Review" (1953) 1 *UCLA L. Rev.* 1.

[25] Earl Warren, "The Northwestern University Law Review Begins Its Fifty-First Year of Publication" (1956) 51 *Northwestern Univ. L. Rev.* 1.

[26] Earl Warren, "Upon the Tenth Anniversary of the *U.C.L.A. Law Review*" (1962) 10 *UCLA L. Rev.* 1.

[27] Roger J. Traynor, "To the Right Honourable Law Reviews" (1962) 10 *UCLA L. Rev.* 3 at 10.

[28] Frank K. Richardson, "Law Reviews and the Courts" (1983) 5 *Whittier L. Rev.* 385 at 392.

[29] Warren, *supra* n. 25, p.1. See also Fuld, *supra* n. 23, pp.917–18.

Appeals claimed in 1935, "I have a feeling of satisfaction which I am sure is justified when we remember that these students come to the law with fresh impressionable minds, sensitive to right and wrong and to any act of injustice".[30]

One could hardly claim, in light of the above quotations, that American judges have been reluctant to acknowledge the initiatives of academics and other legal commentators. Yet do these quotations show that American judicial thought is strongly influenced by the works of academic lawyers? The difficulty with answering this question unequivocally in the affirmative is that much of the encomium rings hollow. The statement that "it is difficult to describe the judge's bliss when he discovers a law review article affirming an opinion that he wrote for the court"[31] might lead some readers to conclude that said judge ought to get out more often. Certainly we might question whether the statement is wholly sincere. Likewise, it is difficult to treat particularly seriously a judge's reflections on the value of legal scholarship when he urges his audience at the law review banquet to "relax and try to enjoy some congratulations" as he sets about "tip[ping his] hat to the law reviews of this country for quietly providing light which helps keep the common law on the right trail".[32] The fact is that all of the quotations in the previous paragraph are taken from presentations which were intended to celebrate the institution of the law review—inaugural addresses, anniversary lectures, after-dinner speeches and the like. It is not particularly surprising to find these judges making the sorts of claims which we have noted above; on such occasions it would most likely be inappropriate not to make the right noises before one's hosts. But the crucial point is that, in such situations, the dominance of etiquette places in doubt the sincerity of the message.

The sincerity of the message is placed in doubt because judges appear, in the illustrations above, to be playing to their audiences. But the fact that the message is being conveyed insincerely does not mean that it must be wrong. Might these judges be presenting sugary versions of what is in fact a true state of affairs? It seems unlikely that this is the case. Judicial expressions of caution and scepticism with regard to American law review literature can be traced back to the early part of

[30] Frederick Evan Crane, "Law School Reviews and the Courts" (1935) 4 *Fordham L. Rev*. 1 at 2.

[31] Fuld, *supra* n. 23, p.916.

[32] Richardson, *supra* n. 28, p.386. The student editors found the judge's comments "to be a great inspiration to all law reviews in their endeavor to provide the legal community with guidance in current developments of the law" (*ibid*., p.385).

the twentieth century. Although Oliver Wendell Holmes contributed a great deal to the law reviews of his era and was not wholly averse to citing periodical literature in his opinions, he tended to look askance at the student contributions to those reviews.[33] "[T]here is an aggravation", he wrote to Frederick Pollock in 1906, "in seeing an unauthoritative person adopt the semi dogmatic judicial tone about his betters—something of what I feel when by chance I see the comments of the youth in the *Harv. Law Rev.*".[34] Chief Justice Charles Hughes recalls Holmes "refer[ring] somewhat scornfully to the 'notes' in law school reviews" as "the 'work of boys' ".[35] Hughes's predecessor as Chief Justice of the Supreme Court, William Howard Taft, frowned upon the judicial citation of even academic contributions to the law reviews and "chided his colleagues (principally Holmes, Brandeis, and Stone) for the 'undignified' use of law review material in their dissents".[36]

One often finds, even among judges who are receptive to law review literature, significant degrees of reserve. "Speaking for the bench", Judge Hoffman of the Northern District Court of Illinois remarked in 1956, "the articles and notes edited and written in the law schools . . . are very welcome additions to the literature of the law".[37] Yet the law reviews often fail the bench in "their tendency to give a disproportionate amount of attention to the appellate courts".[38] In voicing this complaint, Hoffman echoed another judge, Jerome Frank, who, in reviewing a volume of Cardozo's extra-judicial writings, lamented that the latter, "by restricting the judicial process to the appellate courts,

[33] Newland, *supra* n. 14, p.6, claims that Holmes, throughout all of his Supreme Court opinions, cited law journal literature only twice.

[34] See Holmes to Pollock, 6 Sept. 1906, in M. DeWolfe Howe (ed.), *The Pollock-Holmes Letters: Correspondence of Sir Frederick Pollock and Mr Justice Holmes 1874–1932*, 2 vols., (Cambridge, Cambridge University Press, 1942), I, p.133. In the same vein, see also Holmes to Pollock, 13 August 1906, in *ibid.*, I, p.131; and Holmes to Pollock, 7 March 1909, in *ibid.*, I, p.152.

[35] Hughes, *supra* n. 21, p.737; and cf. John Jay McKelvey, "The Law School Review, 1887–1937" (1937) 50 *Harvard L. Rev.* 868 at 880.

[36] Johnson, *supra* n. 14, p.133. See also Alpheus Thomas Mason, *William Howard Taft: Chief Justice* (New York, Simon and Schuster, 1964), pp.268–9. Hughes succeeded Taft as Chief Justice on the latter's death in 1930. In his later years as Chief Justice, Taft became generally irritated by Holmes and Brandeis because of their tendency to join in dissent on constitutional issues. See G. Edward White, *Justice Oliver Wendell Holmes: Law and the Inner Self* (New York, Oxford University Press, 1993), pp.462, 555 n. 128.

[37] Julius Hoffman, "Law Reviews and the Bench" (1956) 51 *Northwestern Univ. L. Rev.* 17.

[38] *Ibid.*, p.19.

presented a picture of the workings of our court system as, in the main, just, reliable, and steady".[39] For Frank, Cardozo's mistake was to pay no attention to "the huge measure of discretion vested in juries and trial judges with respect to the facts" in any particular case.[40] This mistake, Frank claimed, is more commonly made by "the bookish lawyer" who, "[b]eing weak in his experience of the way facts can be made to appear to the fact-trier other than what they are . . . may too easily neglect the major importance of the effective presentation of the facts".[41] According to Hoffman, not only would the law reviews do well to devote more attention to "many of the problems of fact finding and fact determination by the trial court", but it is also the case more generally that "a large group of readers would like to have the reviews devote more space to technical matters".[42] "[I]t might be well for the review editors to consider the proposition", he concludes, "that an academic exercise is not entirely debased when it produces practical results".[43]

In the closing decades of the twentieth century, a number of American judges were to be found reiterating this last proposition. The most famous instance of reiteration is Harry Edwards's article lamenting how "many law schools . . . have abandoned their proper place, by emphasizing abstract theory at the expense of practical scholarship and pedagogy".[44] We will consider this article later. For the moment it will suffice to emphasize that, in expressing this lament, Edwards was not alone. Although "I look to law review articles . . . for a sense of the direction of the law and how the case before us fits within it", wrote Judge Judith Kaye in 1989, "I am disappointed not to find more in the reviews that is of value and pertinence to our cases . . . The concern that academics are writing for each other is indeed well founded".[45] For one District of Columbia circuit judge, writing in 1992, "many of our law reviews are dominated by the rather exotic offerings of increasingly out-of-touch faculty members".[46] Richard Posner, who combines the roles of judge and academic, has been critical of certain of the

[39] Jerome Frank, "Cardozo and the Upper Court Myth" (1948) 13 *Law and Contemporary Problems* 369 at 374.

[40] *Ibid*., p.382.

[41] Jerome Frank, "What Courts Do in Fact" (1932) 26 *Illinois L. Rev*. 645, 761 at 763.

[42] Hoffman, *supra* n. 37, p.20.

[43] *Ibid*.

[44] Edwards, *supra* n. 3, p.34.

[45] Judith S. Kaye, "One Judge's View of Academic Law Review Writing" (1989) 39 *Jnl. Leg. Educ*. 313 at 319–20.

[46] *United States of America* v. *$639,558* 955 F.2d. 712, 722 (1992) (Silberman J., concurring).

arguments, and of the lack of methodology, employed in Edwards's article. Among other things, Posner argues, Edwards exaggerates the undervaluation of doctrinal scholarship in American law schools and underestimates the extent to which non-doctrinal scholarship, such as economic analysis of law, Bayesian probability theory and feminist jurisprudence, has influenced legal practice and decision-making.[47] Yet even Posner believes that Edwards "is . . . right to note a shift away from doctrinal scholarship at the leading law schools"[48] and that much of the non-doctrinal scholarship which appears in the non-peer reviewed law journals is poorly conceived and executed.[49]

It might be argued here that bad publicity is better than no publicity. Numerous twentieth-century American judges paid tribute to the research which emanated from the law schools. Other such judges offered rather more reserved estimations. In one way or another, legal research received judicial acknowledgement. As was noted in Chapter 2, negligible work tends not to be criticized but ignored, and to be criticized might itself be an indication that one has made an impact. The difficulty with this argument in this particular context is that judicial recognition of academic initiative appears not to translate into influence. Some of the recognition, we have seen, seems platitudinous; those judges who discuss legal scholarship critically, furthermore, appear for the most part to be saying that while they are willing to be influenced by academics, the style of work which many of those academics produce will not influence them. "[T]he writings of law professors", Atiyah and Summers write, "influence judges", and "the leading American law schools have been, and continue to be, major sources of basic ideas and bodies of knowledge that shape the legal system".[50] If one digs beneath this assertion and considers what American judges have had to say about academic writing, one finds that although, in general terms, it is a reasonable assertion to make, the influence of such writing on judicial thought is sometimes more perceived than real and, from the perspective of some judges, is not as extensive as it ought to be. In the third section of this chapter, we will return to and develop

[47] See generally Richard A. Posner, *Overcoming Law* (Cambridge, Mass., Harvard University Press, 1995), pp.91–101; also Richard A. Posner, *The Problematics of Moral and Legal Theory* (Cambridge, Mass., Belknap Press, 1999), pp.299–303.

[48] Posner, *Overcoming Law*, *supra* n. 47, p.94.

[49] *Ibid.*, p.98.

[50] P. S. Atiyah and Robert S. Summers, *Form and Substance in Anglo-American Law: A Comparative Study of Legal Reasoning, Legal Theory, and Legal Institutions* (Oxford, Clarendon Press, 1987), pp. 401, 404.

this general observation. In the next section, we will shift perspective and consider how the relationship between academic writing and the courts has been viewed within the American law schools. We will see that within these schools, the prevalent assumption for the best part of the twentieth century has been that the work of legal academics complements and influences the work of judges.

ACADEMICS ON SCHOLARSHIP

It was noted at the outset of the last section that American courts have, as compared with those in England, traditionally been more willing to treat as authority the works of living commentators. Although this is the case, reliance on scholarship by American judges has not always been regarded with approval. "[J]udicial decisions are the only sources and the sole authoritative evidences of the unwritten law", wrote W. M. Lile in 1919.[51] "[N]o textbook or commentary can ever be other than what we term in the law of evidence second-hand or hearsay testimony",[52] notwithstanding "the growing tendency of the bar and the courts to elevate the secondary writer to the high place of a law-giver, co-equal with that of the judges themselves".[53] In a paper presented in 1929 to the meeting of the Association of American Law Schools, Maggs claimed that the American courts of that period were not particularly inclined to rely explicitly on academic writings. "The extent to which law review articles and notes have influenced judges in reaching decisions and/or in giving written reasons for decisions", he reported, "cannot be ascertained. The ideas and the citations in briefs of counsel are often drawn, without acknowledgment in the brief, from law review material".[54] As with Lile, none the less, Maggs observed that judges were becoming ever more appreciative of legal commentary emanating from the law schools. Maggs's analysis of all of the American law reports published between 1928 and 1929 "reveals that 61 out of approximately 850 judges, in 80 out of approximately 30,000 cases, cited 161 law review articles and notes from 27 different law reviews".[55]

[51] W. M. Lile, "The Exaltation of Secondary Authority" (1919) n.s. 14 *Bench and Bar* 53.

[52] *Ibid.*, p.54.

[53] *Ibid.*, p.58.

[54] Douglas B. Maggs, "Concerning the Extent to Which the Law Review Contributes to the Development of the Law" (1930) 3 *Southern Calif. L. Rev.* 181 at 187.

[55] *Ibid.*, p.188, and see also pp.191–204.

In 1945, in his address to the New York State Bar Association, Lyman Wilson challenged the view that the law reviews were becoming increasingly influential. "If there is anywhere in our land a court which has been unduly influenced by a comment or even by a leading article", he proclaimed, "I have yet to discover that court. On the contrary, many a professor and student, who have labored hard upon a case note, have suffered heartburnings when their scholarly effort has been ignored".[56] Wilson's view ran against the grain of dominant scholarly opinion. "[W]e find at least a limited number of lawyers looking towards the law schools for inspiration", wrote McKelvey in 1937; "[a]nd right here is where the law school review finds its broader usefulness. It becomes the vehicle of thought between legal scholars and the practitioners and judges who can absorb and apply, but have not the time for personal research".[57] As the twentieth century progressed, academics became ever more convinced about the capacity of their writings to influence judicial thought. In 1959, Newland provided data which indicated that, between 1924 and 1956, reliance by the Supreme Court on legal periodicals had increased dramatically.[58] Scurlock's study of 1964, detailing the use of criminal law scholarship in the Supreme Court and three appellate courts, suggested that Newland's data—confined as they were to the citation of law review literature—did not fully capture the extent to which courts were becoming reliant on academic writings.[59] "To the extent that the present [Supreme] Court is expanding its reliance from the record and decided cases to the inclusion of law review articles and books by legal scholars", Bernstein claimed in 1968, "it is breaking no new ground. Such citations, though perhaps considered daring a half century ago, have been widely used for many years".[60] During the 1965 term, he adds, "[a]lmost half of the

[56] Lyman P. Wilson, "The Law Schools, the Law Reviews and the Courts" (1945) 30 *Cornell L. Q.* 488 at 496.

[57] McKelvey, *supra* n. 35, p.877.

[58] Chester A. Newland, "Legal Periodicals and the United States Supreme Court" (1959) 7 *Kansas L. Rev.* 477.

[59] "The percentage of cases in which I found citations to scholarly works in the field of criminal law is greater than Professor Newman's [*sic*] overall findings . . . , my 36% against his 26%": John Scurlock, "Scholarship and the Courts" (1964) 32 *Univ. Missouri-Kansas City L. Rev.* 228 at 242. The differences in findings as between these two studies is probably attributable to significant differences in sampling and in methodology. Note also that both studies offer pre-database analyses: consider Scurlock's stark but delightful admission that "my tabulations contain some degree of error. Accuracy in counting is not particularly one of my strong points" (*ibid.*, p.229).

[60] Neil N. Bernstein, "The Supreme Court and Secondary Source Material: 1965 Term" (1968) 57 *Georgetown L. J.* 55 at 66.

written opinions [of the Court] contained some secondary citations, and each such opinion made an average of four secondary references".[61] "The number of citations to legal periodicals" in Supreme Court opinions, according to Daniels, "multiplies by a factor of nearly ten between the 1940 and 1978 terms".[62]

In short, one study after another reinforces the message that, throughout the twentieth century, American judges became ever more willing to cite legal periodicals.[63] In his analysis of the citations of the California Supreme Court during 1950, John Henry Merryman had seen no reason to draw attention to judicial references to law review materials. With the exception of Justice Traynor, the members of that Court were not generally inclined to cite such literature.[64] In his later study of the citation practices of the same Court during the years 1950, 1960 and 1970, however, Merryman noted that judicial citations of legal periodicals had "risen dramatically, from 87 in 1950 to 164 in 1970".[65] Why should this have happened? Between 1950 and 1970, he observed, the number of cases potentially reviewable by the Court greatly expanded while the number of cases heard significantly declined. This naturally led the Court to be more circumspect in choosing its cases, which in turn led "to a concentration on new problems—those of great social importance and those at the growing edge of the law"; to a concentration, in short, on "the sort of law the legal periodicals rejoice in".[66]

It is noticeable that most of the analyses referred to above are concerned only with citations. As was noted in Chapter 2, although citations are often the best proxy that we have for assessing influence, they may offer an incomplete or distorted picture. Within the American law schools, for example, the Matthew effect tends to loom large. Just as

[61] *Ibid.*, p.79.

[62] Daniels, *supra* n. 4, p.15.

[63] See further Mary Anne Bobinski, "Citation Sources and the New York Court of Appeals" (1985) 34 *Buffalo L. Rev.* 965 at 998–1000.

[64] See John Henry Merryman, "The Authority of Authority: What the California Supreme Court Cited in 1950" (1954) 6 *Stanford L. Rev.* 613 at 656–62. During 1950, the California Supreme Court cited law review materials on 87 occasions. Almost one-half (43) of these citations were made by Justice Traynor. Among Traynor's colleagues, Justice Carter produced the second-highest number of such citations (16).

[65] John Henry Merryman, "Toward a Theory of Citations: An Empirical Study of the Citation Practice of the California Supreme Court in 1950, 1960, and 1970" (1977) 50 *Southern Calif. L. Rev.* 381 at 405.

[66] *Ibid.*, p.407; and cf. Robert A. Kagan, Bliss Cartwright, Lawrence M. Friedman and Stanton Wheeler, "The Evolution of State Supreme Courts" (1978) 76 *Michigan L. Rev.* 961 at 991–3.

the most prestigious law schools dominate the production of the nation's law professorate,[67] so too the law reviews of those schools are cited far more frequently by law professors than are all other academic-legal publications.[68] There is evidence that judges too, in so far as they are inclined to cite academic writings, tend to rely on the elite journals.[69] The fact that these journals acquire the lion's share of judicial citations may well indicate that they are the academic-legal authorities which most influence the courts. Alternatively it may indicate that judges, like academics, are often attracted to badges of distinction and that, when judges rely on academic opinion, they generally prefer to be seen relying on a recognized name rather than on a relative unknown. More plausibly, the operation of the Matthew effect might in this instance be partially attributable to the initiatives of law clerks: that is, "the exceptional number of citations to the 'elite' reviews may be due, in part, to the fact that judicial clerks"—most of whom hail from the most prestigious institutions—"are likely to cite to their own law schools' journals".[70]

[67] See Robert J. Borthwick and Jordan R. Schau, "Gatekeepers of the Profession: An Empirical Profile of the Nation's Law Professors" (1991) 25 *Univ. Michigan Jnl. of Law Reform* 191 at 226–36.

[68] See Olavi Maru, "Measuring the Impact of Legal Periodicals" [1976] *Am. Bar Foundation Research Jnl.* 227; Scott Finet, "The Most Frequently Cited Law Reviews and Legal Periodicals" (1989) 9 *Legal Reference Services Quarterly* 227; and James Leonard, "Seein' the Cites: A Guided Tour of Citation Patterns in Recent American Law Review Articles" (1990) 34 *St. Louis Univ. L. J.* 181. It also appears to be the case that most of the articles published in the elite law school journals are written by professors at the elite schools: see The Executive Board, "Chicago-Kent Law Review Faculty Scholarship Survey" (1989) 65 *Chicago-Kent L. Rev.* 195; Colleen M. Cullen and S. Randall Kalberg, "Chicago-Kent Law Review Faculty Scholarship Survey" (1995) 70 *Chicago-Kent L. Rev.* 1445 at 1456–9. Note that this is a context in which the Matthew effect can prove to be a particularly damning effect. As Ayres and Vars argue, "[a]rticles in elite law reviews with few citations . . . are more likely to be of low quality. Finding that a *Harvard Law Review* article has many fewer cites than other articles in the same subject area is hard to square with a hypothesis of excellence": Ian Ayres and Fredrick E. Vars, "Determinants of Citations to Articles in Elite Law Reviews" (2000) 29 *J. Leg. Studs.* 427 at 429.

[69] See Richard A. Mann, "The Use of Legal Periodicals by Courts and Journals" (1986) 26 *Jurimetrics Jnl.* 400; Louis J. Sirico, Jr. and Jeffrey B. Margulies, "The Citing of Law Reviews by the Supreme Court: An Empirical Study" (1986) 34 *UCLA L. Rev.* 131 at 132–4; and Deborah J. Merritt and Melanie Putnam, "Judges and Scholars: Do Courts and Scholarly Journals Cite the Same Law Review Articles?" (1996) 71 *Chicago-Kent L. Rev.* 871. The latter study provides some evidence that even though, as compared with academics, American courts frequently tend to rely upon the same elite journals, they will often not be relying upon the same writings in those journals.

[70] Max Stier, Kelly M. Klaus, Dan L. Bagatell and Jeffrey J. Rachlinski, "Law Review Usage and Suggestions for Improvement: A Survey of Attorneys, Professors, and Judges" (1992) 44 *Stanford L. Rev.* 1467 at 1474; and see also Sirico and Margulies, *supra* n. 69, pp.133–4.

Other possible forms of distortion are identifiable in this context. We have already observed how some judges, in lauding the law reviews, actually raise suspicions that the materials in those reviews might not be particularly influential and that citations may at times reflect not influence but the paying of lip service. American judges may sometimes rely for their citation-sources on the briefs of counsel.[71] It is well known that many of them delegate the task of footnoting relevant academic and other sources to their clerks. Where judges do such things, it would be wrong to assume that the academic literature cited must have influenced judicial thought and decision-making. Some citation analyses indicate that judges who were formerly law professors—Roger Traynor is a good illustration[72]—tend significantly to affect the data because they are disproportionately high citers of academic literature.[73] It should be borne in mind, furthermore, that while various late-twentieth century academic lawyers were attesting to their ever-increasing ability to get cited in courts, certain judges were lamenting the fact that too much modern legal scholarship simply will not, indeed is not intended to, influence them. Scurlock observed as early as 1964 that, although academic influence was on the increase, "[p]ossibly some of the current scholarship devoted to the areas commonly within the reach of judicial cognizance is too futuristic or utopian for ready acceptance."[74] We have seen already that a number of American judges have voiced much the same sentiment. In the next section we will see how, during the later decades of the last century, this sentiment intensified.

[71] It is also worth noting that American academic lawyers may sometimes influence judicial decision-making through the writing of *amicus curiae* briefs. Although the filing of such briefs—which were fairly rare during the early decades of the twentieth century—has become ever more common, evidence that they have much impact on judicial outcomes is in short supply: see Joseph D. Kearney and Thomas W. Merrill, "The Influence of Amicus Curiae Briefs on the Supreme Court" (2000) 148 *Univ. Pennsylvania L. Rev.* 743 at 767–74.

[72] See Merryman, *supra* n. 64, pp.662, 667; and note also G. Edward White, "Roger Traynor" (1983) 69 *Virginia L. Rev.* 1381 at 1384 ("Traynor's academic roots affected his attitude towards judging: he wrote not only for practitioners and affected parties but for an audience of commentators. For him there was no significant difference between the academic and judicial worlds, just as there was no significant difference in the weight of academic or judicial authorities").

[73] Owing, one assumes, to the fact that they are—as compared with judges who have not worked as law professors—more likely to be familiar with and able to find their way around relevant academic literature.

[74] Scurlock, *supra* n. 59, pp.261–2.

WHAT IS TO BE DONE?

"American jurisprudence", one commentator observed in 1983, "has recurringly fallen into fits of obsession with the judiciary to the neglect of other aspects of the huge edifice of our legal system".[75] Sixty to seventy per cent of American law review articles, another observer claimed around this time, are written with the requirements of the legal profession in mind.[76] Typical of the articles which fall into this category is the "case analysis", the apparent purpose of this genre being to provide "a research aid for lawyers . . . and for the judges before whom those lawyers appear".[77] Although a considerable amount of American legal scholarship is addressed to the courts, Rubin has argued, it rarely provides judges with the sort of normative and empirical guidance that they are likely to need: academic lawyers tend to "argue with the court's reasoning in the same speculative and delimited terms the court itself employs, rather than constituting an independent research program . . . What judges need is not an iteration of their own approach, but assistance in those areas where the demands of that approach have outrun their institutional and conceptual resources".[78]

Whether such observations are well-founded—and there are those who would contend that they are not[79]—is not the issue here. What is of interest is the fact that, in the late decades of the twentieth century, academic lawyers were offering such observations. Was it not the case that legal scholarship was influencing the courts? Had not various citation analyses, some of which were considered in the previous section, indicated as much? Writing for judges may not be the most ambitious scholarly agenda in the world, but, if this writing makes an impact, why lament the fact? In the late 1950s, the citation of legal periodical literature in Supreme Court antitrust opinions provoked criticism of

[75] Graham Hughes, "The Great American Legal Scholarship Bazaar" (1983) 33 *Jnl. Leg. Educ*. 424 at 427.

[76] Mark Tushnet, "Legal Scholarship: Its Causes and Cure" (1981) 90 *Yale L. J*. 1205 at 1208.

[77] *Ibid*., p.1209.

[78] Edward L. Rubin, "The Practice and Discourse of Legal Scholarship" (1988) 86 *Michigan L. Rev*. 1835 at 1890–1.

[79] Consider, for example, the nuanced response to Rubin presented by Meir Dan-Cohen, "Listeners and Eavesdroppers: Substantive Legal Theory and Its Audience" (1992) 63 *Univ. Colorado L. Rev*. 569 especially at 588–91.

the Court within Congress.[80] By the 1980s, the influence of neo-classical law and economics scholarship on antitrust decision-making in the courts of appeals and the Supreme Court was not only widely acknowledged but was also, in some quarters, being vigorously encouraged.[81] Law and economics testifies to the influence of academics on courts. Might it not be argued that the initiatives of lawyer-economists, for all that they do not suit everyone's tastes, affirm the basic point that jurists can make some sort of difference? And is not this ability to make a difference a cause for celebration?

To answer any of the above questions in an unqualifiedly positive fashion would be naive. Many American legal academics have resisted treating influence as a desirable end in itself. Academic influence on courts may come at a price: an emphasis on writing for the judiciary might—this is the point of the quotation at the beginning of this section—detract from other worthwhile goals. No influence may sometimes be preferable to bad influence: hence Robert Gordon's remark that he does not deny the pervasive influence of law and economics, but only wishes it were not so.[82] Some academic lawyers have even remained unconvinced that scholarship does have much influence over judges. A study dealing with Supreme Court citations to academic literature between 1971 and 1983 found that, during that period, citations to such literature declined significantly.[83] The authors of the study suggested that the decline may be attributable to the increasing tendency of academics to write literature which is likely to be of interest only to other academics, rather than to the bar or the bench.[84] During the 1990s the belief that legal scholarship is, so far as the work of judges is concerned, of little or no relevance became more prevalent. "[T]he academic practice of writing for judges", Schlag claimed in 1992,

[80] See Chester A. Newland, "The Supreme Court and Legal Writing: Learned Journals as Vehicles of An Anti-Antitrust Lobby?" (1959) 48 *Georgetown L. J.* 105. The criticism very much echoed the political climate of the period. According to Congressman Wright Patman, the Supreme Court was acting inappropriately in its "consideration of unknown, unrecognized and nonauthoritative text books, Law Review articles, and other writings of propaganda artists and lobbyists" (1957) 103 *Congressional Record* 16160 (cited after Newland, *ibid.*, p.105). On an earlier occasion Patman had excoriated judicial reliance "not upon the law but upon pro-Communist agitators and enemies of our system of government" (1955) 101 *Congressional Record* 7124 (cited after Newland, *ibid.*).

[81] See generally Neil Duxbury, *Patterns of American Jurisprudence* (Oxford, Clarendon Press, 1995), pp.358–63.

[82] Robert W. Gordon, "Lawyers, Scholars, and the 'Middle Ground'" (1993) 91 *Michigan L. Rev.* 2075 at 2084.

[83] Sirico and Margulies, *supra* n. 69, p.134.

[84] See *ibid.*, p.135.

"increasingly appears as a degraded art-form used to communicate with personas who are not listening in order to achieve nothing very much whatsoever".[85] "By and large, neither judges nor any other bureaucratic decision makers are listening to academic advice that they are not already prepared to believe."[86]

Throughout the twentieth century, as we have seen, a considerable amount of literature was produced, by both judges and academics, either arguing or attempting to demonstrate that many judges could not do without their law reviews and that academic analysis was becoming ever more highly regarded as a secondary legal source. Yet, by the end of the century, various law professors appeared to want to spoil the party. In England throughout this period, as will become clear in Chapter 5, academic lawyers had often felt starved of judicial attention. American academic lawyers appeared to be receiving this attention—certainly much more of it than were their English counterparts—and yet some of them were claiming that the attention was unwelcome, or that it was not the right sort of attention or even that they were as normatively redundant as were the English. What was happening?

It is tempting to assume that American academic lawyers were being churlish. One would expect the land of plenty to produce its share of spoilt brats; possibly these academics were simply responding with bad grace to their good fortune. For at least two reasons, however, this suggestion seems unconvincing. Ever since the realist era, first of all, American legal academics have used the law school review as a mirror in which to scrutinize themselves. While the review, mainly owing to student editing, too often fails to discourage vanity, it rarely prevents law professors from being brutally honest about themselves when they are so inclined. Thus it is that the law review article sometimes takes the form of a confessional.[87] Fred Rodell, renowned in his time for combining honesty and vanity, used the pages of a law review to reflect critically on the genre and also to declare that he would never again write an article for such a review (a promise he failed to keep).[88] Within

[85] Pierre Schlag, "Writing for Judges" (1992) 63 *Univ. Colorado L. Rev*. 419 at 422.

[86] Schlag, *supra* n. 2, p.70.

[87] See, e.g., Sanford Levinson, "The Audience for Constitutional Meta-Theory (Or, Why, and To Whom, Do I Write the Things I Do?)" (1992) 63 *Univ. Colorado L. Rev*. 389 (author confessing that he does not write with judges in mind because he cannot imagine that judges would be interested in anything that he has to say).

[88] See Fred Rodell, "Goodbye to Law Reviews" (1936) 23 *Virginia L. Rev*. 38. On his failure to stick to his word, see Neil Duxbury, "In the Twilight of Legal Realism: Fred Rodell and the Limits of Legal Critique" (1991) 11 *Oxf. Jnl. Leg. Studs*. 354 at 374.

the American law review more or less anything goes, and it would be surprising if we did *not* find academics doubting their ability, or questioning the point of trying, to influence judicial decision-making.

The second point to note is that those modern law professors who do raise such doubts and questions tend to be querulous and reflective rather than cynical and dismissive. What do legal scholars do? Should we expect them to influence, or even try to influence, judges? Should we be surprised when their work fails to be uninfluential? While much of the literature which addresses such questions is rather gloomy, it is usually serious and rarely boorish.[89] In the late 1960s, one of the classic soul-searching articles of American legal thought raised the question of why it should be that American law professors are so willing and confident to wander into disciplinary domains within which they have no professional training.[90] Although there is no doubt that philosophical study can reveal important insights about law it seems odd that many of these professors, despite having no formal qualifications in philosophy, should undertake projects of remarkable philosophical ambition.[91] "[F]or legal academics", Carrington has argued, "there is often a choice to be made between work that can and may be applied usefully to current public issues and work that is intellectually more ambitious, more personally gratifying, and more likely to win recognition among academicians".[92] There is no exaggeration in the claim that more or less every theoretical trend finds its place in the American law school.[93] Although

[89] Though it is possible to find a fair number of law professors excoriating their own profession: see, e.g., Bryden, *supra* n. 2, *passim*; Robert L. Bard, "Legal Scholarship and the Professional Responsibility of Law Professors" (1984) 19 *Connecticut L. Rev.* 731 at 732 ("[M]ost new law professors are incompetent to do valuable legal scholarship"); James W. Ely, Jr., "Through a Crystal Ball: Legal Education—Its Relation to the Bench, Bar, and University Community" (1986) 21 *Tulsa L. J.* 650 at 654 ("We know that most law review articles have a low readership and that even academic lawyers regard much of the literature as worthless"); and John Henry Schlegel, "A Certain Narcissism; a Slight Unseemliness" (1992) 63 *Univ. Colorado L. Rev.* 595 ("I write from the firm conviction that we do a piss-poor job of preparing students to be lawyers and that we could do one hell of a better job at this practical task, which I take to be the primary job of a law school").

[90] See Thomas F. Bergin, "The Law Teacher: A Man Divided Against Himself" (1968) 54 *Virginia L. Rev.* 637 at 647.

[91] Jules L. Coleman, "Legal Theory and Practice" (1995) 83 *Georgetown L. J.* 2579; and cf. Lubet, *supra* n. 2, *passim*.

[92] Carrington, *supra* n. 2, p.802.

[93] See George L. Priest, "The Increasing Division Between Legal Practice and Legal Education" (1988/89) 37 *Buffalo L. Rev.* 681. The observation is not offered cynically. For Priest, the capacity and eagerness of law schools to accommodate new theoretical trends is indicative of intellectual vitality and progress. See also Robert Post, "Legal Scholarship and the Practice of Law" (1992) 63 *Univ. Colorado L. Rev.* 615 at 620–1.

it is unlikely "that much academically fashionable interdisciplinary legal scholarship will ever find application in the corridors of power",[94] such scholarship has become a particularly valuable currency within the academic community itself.[95]

Valued thus, scholarship tends to turn inwards on itself. Thurman Arnold complained as far back as 1935 that American law review writing is too often "known only to the few people who read it for the purpose of writing more of it".[96] Expressions of disquiet concerning the insularity of much legal scholarship, especially at the most prestigious law schools, became especially prevalent in the 1990s. "Legal scholars, most particularly of the elite variety, seem to be more interested in gaining acceptance as participants in the intellectual life of the university than in communicating with other law professors, judges, lawyers, or law students to improve the quality of the practice of law".[97] "At best, elite law schools prepare their top five students to become law professors but fail to prepare the rest of their students to become practicing lawyers."[98] "[A]t the major schools . . . [t]he doctrinal analyst is seldom admired . . . and infrequently appointed."[99] No doubt there is a possibility that such concerns are overstated. One fairly recent survey suggests that approximately three-quarters of what appeared in the law reviews in 1960 was doctrinal or practitioner-oriented scholarship, whereas approximately half of the scholarship published in the reviews of 1985 was of this type.[100] While theoretical research may be a growth industry, it would be wrong to assume that doctrinal work no longer has its producers and consumers.[101] That doctrinalism is still a significant research agenda becomes obvious if one shifts one's focus away from the contents of the most prestigious reviews; indeed, the study noted above concludes, those who complain about the growing irrelevance of legal scholarship to the needs of practitioners would do

[94] Carrington, *supra* n. 2, p.802.

[95] See Richard A. Posner, "The Decline of Law as an Autonomous Discipline: 1962–1987" (1987) 100 *Harvard L. Rev*. 761 at 766–72.

[96] Thurman W. Arnold, "Apologia for Jurisprudence" (1935) 44 *Yale L. J*. 729.

[97] Banks McDowell, "The Audiences for Legal Scholarship" (1990) 40 *Jnl. Leg. Educ*. 261 at 275.

[98] Johnson, *supra* n. 2, p.1252.

[99] Graham C. Lilly, "Law Schools Without Lawyers? Winds of Change in Legal Education" (1995) 81 *Virginia L. Rev*. 1421 at 1436.

[100] Michael J. Saks, Howard Larsen and Carol J. Hodne, "Is There a Growing Gap Among Law, Law Practice, and Legal Scholarship?: A Systematic Comparison of Law Review Articles One Generation Apart" (1996) 30 *Suffolk Univ. L. Rev*. 353 at 370.

[101] See also Posner, *supra* n. 47, pp.94–5; Gordon, *supra* n. 82, pp.2099–101.

well to utilize a wider range of law journals.[102] Within this exhortation, of course, there is an implicit acknowledgement of the problem: the perceived disjunction between legal scholarship and legal practice is partly explicable by reference to the Matthew effect. The elite journals show a preference for publishing non-doctrinal work, and those are the journals which attract the most attention: hence the apparent disjunction.

The most significant lament about this disjunction was Harry Edwards's article of 1992. "[T]he legal scholar's work", according to Edwards, "must be valuable. 'Personal fascination' is not a justification for scholarship, of any kind".[103] Opportunities for legal academics to demonstrate their value are abundant. They may prove their worth by synthesizing information ("a high quality, 'practical' article or Note is immensely useful to the judge")[104] and by offering critical reflection ("[t]he article writer should serve as a 'judge of judges' ").[105] "[A] good 'practical' scholar gives due weight to cases, statutes and other authoritative texts, but also employs theory to criticize doctrine, to resolve problems that doctrine leaves open, and to propose changes in the law or in systems of justice."[106] Edwards's "principal fear" was "that some law professors *cum* theorists have forgotten the obvious"[107]—*viz.*, that "academicians and practitioners have a joint obligation to serve the system of justice".[108] Evidence that this fear was well-founded was fairly abundant, he believed, throughout the better American law schools. "[M]any 'elite' law faculties in the United States now have significant contingents of 'impractical' scholars, who are 'disdainful' of the practice of law".[109] "Our law reviews are now full of mediocre interdisciplinary articles. Too many law professors are ivory tower dilettantes."[110] While doctrinal scholarship is being "discouraged"[111] and "disdained . . . we now see 'law professors' hired from graduate schools, wholly lacking in legal experience or training, who use the law school as a bully pulpit from which to pour scorn upon the legal

[102] See Saks *et al.*, *supra* n. 100, pp.374–5.
[103] Edwards, *supra* n. 3, p.56.
[104] *Ibid.*, p.46.
[105] *Ibid.*, p.45. Note here how Edwards echoes Fuld: see text accompanying n. 23, *supra*.
[106] Edwards, *supra* n. 3, p.35.
[107] *Ibid.*, p.66.
[108] *Ibid.*, p.38.
[109] *Ibid.*, p.35.
[110] *Ibid.*, p.36.
[111] *Ibid.*, p.51.

profession".[112] "My view", Edwards concludes, "is that if law schools continue to stray from their principal mission of *professional* scholarship and training, the disjunction between legal education and the legal profession will grow and society will be the worse for it".[113]

Edwards's article certainly hit a nerve. Academics, practitioners and judges produced responses which were variously supportive, conciliatory and (most often of all) critical.[114] Edwards had attempted to substantiate his arguments by quoting from written responses to an informal survey which he had circulated to his former law clerks. While he conceded that "[t]he survey did not purport to draw statistically reliable data",[115] he relied heavily on it. Few critics minced their words.[116] Although, in follow-up essays, Edwards emphasized that "[n]ot all 'impractical' teaching and scholarship is bad"[117] and conceded that he "may . . . have overstated the negative influence of 'impractical' scholars and scholarship",[118] he remained essentially defiant in the face of those who questioned his basic thesis. Taking sides in the dispute is not the objective of the discussion here. Far more interesting for our purposes is the very fact that Edwards's article should have proved so provocative. As Edwards himself noted, and as we have already seen, he was not the first commentator to bemoan a growing gap between the objectives of scholarship and the requirements of lawyers and

[112] Edwards, *supra* n. 3, p.37.

[113] *Ibid*., p.41.

[114] For support see, e.g., Paul D. Reingold, "Harry Edwards' Nostalgia" (1993) 91 *Michigan L. Rev*. 1998–2009; and Andrew Burrows, *Understanding the Law of Obligations: Essays on Contract, Tort and Restitution* (Oxford, Hart, 1998), pp 112–14, 118–19. For conciliatory efforts see, e.g., George L. Priest, "The Growth of Interdisciplinary Research and the Industrial Structure of the Production of Legal Ideas: A Reply to Judge Edwards" (1993) 91 *Michigan L. Rev*. 1929; and James Boyd White, "Law Teachers' Writing" (1993) 91 *Michigan L. Rev*. 1970; and for critique see, e.g., Louis H. Pollack, "The Disjunction Between Judge Edwards and Professor Priest" (1993) 91 *Michigan L. Rev*. 2113; Paul Brest, "Plus ça change" (1993) 91 *Michigan L. Rev*. 1945; John Gava, "Scholarship and Community" (1994) 16 *Sydney L. Rev*. 443 at 444–9; and Brian R. Cheffins, "Using Legal Theory to Study Law: A Company Law Perspective" (1999) 58 *C.L.J*. 197 at 203–6.

[115] Edwards, *supra* n. 3, p.42.

[116] See, e.g., Sanford Levinson, "Judge Edwards' Indictment of 'Impractical' Scholars: The Need for a Bill of Particulars" (1993) 91 *Michigan L. Rev*. 2010 at 2021 ("Judge Edwards' attempt to blame 'impractical' academics for the present ethical state of the legal services industry would be laughable if it were not otherwise so pathetically misleading as a diagnosis of our present discontents").

[117] Harry T. Edwards, "Another 'Postscript' to 'The Growing Disjunction Between Legal Education and the Legal Profession' " (1994) 69 *Washington L. Rev*. 561 at 564.

[118] Harry T. Edwards, "The Growing Disjunction Between Legal Education and the Legal Profession: A Postscript" (1993) 91 *Michigan L. Rev*. 2191 at 2192.

judges.[119] So why all the fuss? Perhaps the answer is that, on this occasion, the concern was being elaborated not by a law professor but by a judge. Although Edwards had served as a professor at Michigan and at Harvard in the 1970s, he had since 1980 sat as Judge of the United States Court of Appeals for the District of Columbia Circuit. His article was primarily an expression not of scholarly disappointment but of judicial expectation. During the twentieth century—this seems to be the gist of Edwards's position—American law professors have been blessed with a judiciary which has often listened to and welcomed their views. Rarely have judges denigrated academic endeavour, regularly have they accorded it significance. Yet the most privileged of those professors have shown themselves to be ethereal, solipsistic, contemptuous of the needs of the profession, unwilling to acknowledge, let alone to return, the compliment paid to them by the bench. The professorate blew their chance, turned up their noses at the invitation to try to make a difference. No matter that this is exaggeration, that many academic lawyers have welcomed and made good use of the invitation. The point is that the hyperbole captures the predicament: since the heady days of Cardozo and Brandeis, American law professors, while they have recognized that influencing judicial thought is a feasible goal, have not always equated the feasible with the desirable.

Thus it is that the sunshine turns to haze. Academic writings can and do influence American judicial decision-making. The fact that judges quite regularly cite academics indicates (even accounting for the role played by law clerks) that academics must be doing something right, that their work is having a degree of impact. Indeed, this very argument is the one most regularly advanced in academic studies of the effect of scholarship on courts. While this argument ought not to be dismissed, it none the less plays down the stream of judicial dissatisfaction which we have witnessed running throughout parts of this chapter. Abundance brings its own insecurities. Within the jurisdiction where courts are indifferent to scholarly lucubration, academics are likely to feast on whatever scraps of attention they might get. In the USA, the courts have made eye-contact with the law schools and smiled. The most glamorous of these law schools, instead of beaming back, have caused consternation by playing cool.

Neither academics nor judges have been reluctant to analyse this distance between the two realms; indeed, the American enthusiasm for

[119] See Edwards, *supra* n. 3, p.34 n. 2.

juristic introspection is phenomenal. In France, to offer a comparison, we almost never find judges articulating their expectations of academics. There it is the judges who have tradionally played cool. Equipped with a basic knowledge of the French legal system, one might consider it a safe conclusion that the influence of academics on the courts within that system must be negligible. Such a conclusion would, in fact, be remarkably shaky.

4

France

"FRENCH SCHOLARS", it is alleged in *The Name of The Rose*, "are notoriously careless about furnishing reliable bibliographical information".[1] French judges, certainly in the higher courts, are notorious for their reluctance to provide much in the way of any information. "[C]ommon law judges still seem to talk to everyone who is prepared to listen (or must listen), German judges only talk to intellectual equals, and French judges (at the highest levels) keep their thoughts to themselves!"[2] The terseness and formality of the French judicial opinion have traditionally militated against the citation of legal scholarship in the higher courts.[3] In the late 1970s an eminent French public prosecutor, Adolphe Touffait, claimed that the law professors who would ever stand a chance of gaining an audience with, and who might ever be cited as authority by, the Cour de cassation could be counted on the fingers of one hand.[4] Yet we ought not to deduce from

[1] Umberto Eco, *The Name of The Rose* (Eng. trans. W. Weaver, London, Secker & Warburg, 1983 [1980]), p.3.

[2] B. S. Markesinis, "Learning from Europe and Learning in Europe", in B. S. Markesinis (ed.), *The Gradual Convergence: Foreign Ideas, Foreign Influences, and English Law on the Eve of the 21st Century* (Oxford, Clarendon Press, 1994), pp.1–32 at 30. In a similar vein, see Hein Kötz, "The Role of the Judge in the Court-Room: The Common Law and Civil Law Compared" [1987] *Tydskrif v. S.-A. Reg.* 35 at 41–2.

[3] See Pierre Mimin, *Le style des jugements (Vocabulaire—Construction—Dialectique—Formes juridiques)* (4th edn., Paris, Librairies Techniques, 1978), p.274. On terseness, see Jean Louis Goutal, "Characteristics of Judicial Style in France, Britain and the U.S.A." (1976) 24 *Am. J. Compar. Law* 43 at 59–60; André Tunc, "Synthèse" (1978) 30 *Rev. Int. Droit Comparé* 5 at 72–4; Pierre Bellet, "La Cour de cassation" (1978) 30 *Rev. Int. Droit Comparé* 193 at 213–15; and B. S. Markesinis, "A Matter of Style" (1994) 110 *L.Q.R.* 607 at 608–9. On the history of the disciplined and constrained manner of explanation in French judicial decision-making, see Tony Sauvel, "Histoire du jugement motivé" (1955) 71 *Revue du Droit Public et de la Science Politique en France et à l'Étranger* 5. For pleas for more explicit and elaborate judicial reasoning, see Adolphe Touffait and André Tunc, "Pour une motivation plus explicite des décisions de justice, notamment de celles de la Cour de cassation" (1974) 72 *Revue trimestrielle de droit civil* 487; and Raymond Lindon, "La motivation des arrêts de la Cour de cassation" (1975) I—Doctrine *La Semaine Juridique* 2681; and on resistance to such pleas, see André Tunc, "Conclusions: La cour suprême idéale" (1978) 30 *Rev. Int. Droit Comparé* 433 at 461–3. Cf. also Michael Wells, "French and American Judicial Opinions" (1994) 19 *Yale Jnl. Int'l Law* 81.

this claim that judicial thought in France has developed without any regard for the opinions of academic lawyers. David remarked in 1948 that academic commentary in England does not influence judges anywhere near as much as it does in France.[5] Since the late nineteenth century, according to Malaurie, a significant number of French judicial decisions, particularly appellate decisions, have been accompanied by formal reasoning "inspired by university opinions".[6] When considering the influence of academic opinion on French judicial thought, he remarks, it is especially important to take account of the distinctive critical function of the *note d'arrêt* or case note.[7] The basic purpose of this chapter is to try to show how case note writing in France has been an influential form of juristic commentary largely because, rather than in spite of, traditional judicial reticence.

HISTORY OF THE *NOTE D'ARRÊT*

The vibrant tradition of case note writing in France might be cited in support of the general view, held by jurists dating back to Gény, that French judges, although they supposedly do nothing of the sort, regularly formulate and develop legal rules.[8] If judges really were incapable of creativity, it would be unlikely that the efforts of the case note writers, the *arrêtistes*, would be considered particularly important or valuable. (How many interesting case notes might be written, after all, about a decision-making procedure which is characterized by formalism and which demands judicial passivity?) In fact, within the French system, case note writing is generally held in high regard. The primary explanation for this is perhaps historical: as is well known, the glossatorial tradition in Roman law—upon which the French *droit civil* is

[4] Adolphe Touffait, "Conclusions d'un practicien" (1978) 30 *Rev. Int. Droit Comparé* 473 at 484. As the highest court in France dealing with private law matters, the Cour de cassation is concerned with the application of the law to the facts as found by lower courts and, more generally, with the general exposition and development of private law.

[5] René David, *Introduction à l'étude du droit privé de l'Angleterre* (Paris, Recueil Sirey, 1948), p.168.

[6] Philippe Malaurie, "Les réactions de la doctrine à la création du droit par les juges: Rapport français" (1980) 31 *Travaux de l'Association Henri Capitant* 81 at 91.

[7] *Ibid.*, p.90.

[8] See François Gény, *Méthode d'interprétation et sources en droit privé positif: Essai critique*, 2 vols. (2nd edn., Paris, L.G.D.J., 1919), II, pp.210–12; Evelyne Serverin, *De la jurisprudence en droit privé: Théorie d'une pratique* (Lyon, Presses universitaires de Lyon, 1985), pp.145–54.

founded—emphasized the role of legal scholarship in the shaping of the law.[9] "[I]t was essentially in the universities that the principles of law emerged between the thirteenth and nineteenth centuries. Only recently has the primacy of doctrinal writing given way to that of enacted law, with the establishment of democratic ideas and the advent of codification".[10] Even in a field such as administrative law—which in France is a largely uncodified, case law subject—there exists a pronounced tradition of case note writing.[11]

The emergence of case note writing as a general phenomenon in France can be traced back to the 1840s, during which decade there were inaugurated a number of journals devoted to the reporting and the analysis of judicial decisions.[12] The first commentaries on cases were published in 1845, with the inception of *Dalloz*. In the early years, such commentaries appeared unattributed (most likely they were written by the editorial team). "Looking through our contemporary collections of legal decisions", Meynial observed in 1904:

> "where the decisions of courts are examined closely by scholars, noting the place that these collections have in our legal education and the editorial role played by our doctrinal jurists, sensing the intimate and daily relations which unite the law schools (*l'École*) and the world of the judge and practitioner (*le Palais*) . . . we could believe that things have always been so and could not be otherwise. In believing as much we would certainly be deluding ourselves. During the first part of the nineteenth century . . . practice and academic commentary ignored each other and each followed its own distinct path. Not until after the Revolution of 1830 did there begin a movement towards rapprochement. Previously, academic commentary was full of scorn for the work of the practitioner, considering it to be the equivalent of unskilled labour . . . Even in 1837 Ledru-Rollin, in his preface to the third edition of the *Journal du Palais*, could lament that the old state of affairs persisted, and in 1840 Devilleneuve, in his new edition of the earliest volumes of *Sirey*, expressed much the same sentiments. It is only after 1852 that

[9] See Harold J. Berman, "The Origins of Western Legal Science" (1977) 90 *Harv. L. Rev*. 894 at 940.

[10] René David and John E. C. Brierley, *Major Legal Systems in the World Today: An Introduction to the Study of Comparative Law* (London, Stevens & Sons, 1978), p.134.

[11] A tradition which, in this instance, can be dated back to the 1890s. See Théodore Fortsakis, *Conceptualisme et empirisme en droit administratif Français* (Paris, L.G.D.J., 1987), pp.109–20.

[12] See Édouard J.-M. Meynial, *Les Recueils d'arrêts et les Arrêtistes* (Extrait du Livre du centennaire du code civil, publié par la Société d'études législatives, Paris, A. Rousseau, 1904), p.25.

> . . . academic commentary gradually begins to play the role of organizer of case law".[13]

The journals which began to appear in the 1840s were usually the joint ventures of academic and practising lawyers, and the case notes which they contained were the product of, and were intended to be of interest to, both constituencies. According to Meynial, the case notes of this period "constituted an especially subtle form of legal literature, capable of being turned by a journal editor into something either dogmatic or practical, while remaining of cardinal interest to both readerships".[14] The fact that, in nineteenth century France, case notes were produced not only by academic but also by practising lawyers—and even, occasionally, by judges—provides, Meynial believes, part of the explanation as to why the worlds of the academic lawyer on the one hand and the practitioner and judge on the other have not, traditionally, been all that far apart. For the basic purpose of case note writing was not only to analyse case law—to try to uncover and explain the rationale behind decisions and to examine how, or if, particular outcomes might be reconciled with those reached in earlier or analogous cases—but also to consider whether existing legal commentary or *doctrine* might indicate how, in the future, judges might advance *la jurisprudence* still further. Thus it is that Meynial ascribed to the efforts of *les arrêtistes* a distinctly constructive, dialectical function: through commentary on cases, academics, practitioners and judges were able to promote the complementary development of *jurisprudence* and *doctrine*, of case law and legal writing. "[C]ase notes", he proclaimed, "represent best and most consistently the movement of case law towards the perspective of doctrinal examination, so that throughout history these two connected forms merge into one . . . Case notes and doctrinal examination . . . will surely become the two most indispensable and powerful instruments for regularizing our entire legal world".[15] Echoing Meynial, Dawson observes that in the French legal context, case notes:

> "perform the same function as a forum for free criticism and exchange of views. Being comments on the cases reported, they address themselves to specific issues, to all the nuances in the facts, to the motives for the decision whether expressed or veiled, and to the possibilities of reconciling results

[13] Meynial, *ibid.*, pp.4–5.
[14] *Ibid.*, p.24.
[15] *Ibid.*, pp.25–6, 31.

with those in earlier cases, by distinctions or otherwise. The analytical note is also expected to assemble all the resources of doctrine, to criticize and evaluate it in its bearing on the specific problem. It is an extremely flexible instrument, expressing the skill, learning, and insight of individual authors but requiring them to address themselves to the interests and needs of practitioners as well as to those of their academic colleagues".[16]

It is worth noting that, in their presentations of French case note writing, both Meynial and Dawson assume the existence of judicial creativity. Indeed, Meynial believed that study of the phenomenon of case note writing revealed the misapprehensions of the representatives of *l'école de l'exégèse* of the nineteenth century, who were of the view that the text of the Civil Code was generally straightforward and uncontroversial and that, in those instances where interpretation was necessary, answers were to be found in the *travaux préparatoires*. The work of *les arrêtistes*, he claims, makes it difficult to take seriously "those early nineteenth century dogmatic jurists who took such a haughty attitude towards practice and who were so deeply convinced of the virtue of the rigid formula of the law".[17] Discussing the principal journal editors and case note writers of the nineteenth century, Meynial observes that both groups operated with the knowledge that what appeared in the journals would sometimes influence the development of case law.[18]

The most prolific and important of the nineteenth century case note writers was the law professor, J.-E. Labbé.[19] Between the appearance of his first case note in 1859 and his death in 1894, Labbé published, mainly in *Sirey*, literally hundreds of influential notes on cases covering more or less the entire spectrum of French private law.[20] "He and others like him", Dawson remarks, "discovered for themselves and revealed to their colleagues the depth, richness, and complexity of the gloss the courts had laid on the codes".[21] This vibrant tradition of French case note writing carried over into the twentieth century.[22]

[16] John P. Dawson, *The Oracles of the Law* (Ann Arbor, University of Michigan Law School, 1968), pp.398–9.

[17] Meynial, *supra* n. 12, pp.31–2.

[18] *Ibid*., pp.26–8.

[19] See, generally, Fernand Baudet, *Labbé arrêtiste; aperçu générale de ses doctrines en droit civil*, thèse pour le doctorat (Sciences Juridiques), Faculté de Droit, Université de Lille, 1908 (publ. Lille, C. Robbe, 1908).

[20] See further Meynial, *supra* n. 12, pp.28–30.

[21] Dawson, *supra* n. 16, p.399.

[22] See, for example, the influential note by the eminent late-nineteenth century commercial lawyer, Charles Lyon-Caen, concerning the contractual obligations of carriers to

Indeed, perhaps the best known instance where case note writing affected a legal outcome is in the case of *Jand'heur* c. *Les Galeries Belfortaises* (1930) in which the Cour de cassation, influenced by the case notes of Saleilles and Josserand, interpreted article 1384 al. 1 (concerning liability for the "deeds of things") as establishing a presumption of *responsibility* on the part of the person who is in control of an inanimate object which has caused harm to another, thereby preventing that person from escaping liability by proving that he was not at fault for the harm done.[23] Josserand in particular had used the medium of the case note essentially to mount a campaign to influence the thinking of the Cour de cassation on the subject of liability for the deeds of things, rather as Sir Frederick Pollock embarked on a crusade to direct the House of Lords away from the position at which it arrived in *Derry* v. *Peek* (see Chapter 5).[24] As another *arrêtiste* noted apropos the *Jand'heur* case, from the perspective of the doctrinal commentator Josserand's success in influencing the thinking of the Cour de cassation was cause for the ultimate "*cri de triomphe*".[25]

Just as Labbé had led the way in the nineteenth century, twentieth century *arrêtistes* such as Josserand, Planiol, Capitant and Waline continued to use the case note as a medium through which to consider the implications and possible shortcomings of, as well as the reasons behind and doctrinal background to, the decisions of courts.[26] The principal art of case note writing, Carbonnier observes, is to consider the exercise as an opportunity to try to influence judicial thought in the future by highlighting, in view of what a court has already decided,

passengers, as reported and discussed in Otto Kahn-Freund, Claudine Lévy and Bernard Rudden, *A Source-book on French Law: Systems—Methods—Outlines of Contract* (2nd edn., Oxford, Clarendon Press, 1979), pp.171–6; and consider also the case note writing career of René Savatier, as celebrated by Jean Carbonnier, "Notes sur des notes d'arrêts: Chronique pour le cinquantième anniversaire de l'entrée du Doyen René Savatier au Dalloz", D. 1970, Chron. 137–9.

[23] Cass. ch. réun. 13 Feb. 1930, rapp. Le Marc'hadour, concl. Matter, 1930 S. Jur. 1. 121. DP 1930 1. 57 (note Ripert), DP 1930 1. 121 (note Esmein). For an English translation of the case, see A. T. von Mehren and J. R. Gordley (eds), *The Civil Law System: An Introduction to the Comparative Study of Law* (2nd edn., Boston, Little, Brown & Co., 1977), pp.629–31. For abridged reprints of the notes by Ripert, Esmein and others on the *Jand'heur* case, see F. H. Lawson, *Negligence in the Civil Law: Introduction and Select Texts* (Oxford, Clarendon Press, 1950), pp.268–79.

[24] See, in particular, Louis Josserand, note DH 1930, Chron. 25–9.

[25] Ripert, *supra* n. 23, p.57.

[26] See further Jean Roche, "Les réactions de la doctrine à la création du droit par les juges: Rapport français" (1980) 31 *Travaux de l'Association Henri Capitant* 555 at 562–4.

alternative outcomes, approaches and lines of reasoning.[27] Thus it is that, in France, the modern case note has provided feedback to the judiciary—a judiciary which is generally responsive to, and sometimes prepared to participate in, academic dialogue.[28]

It is important not to paint too rosy a picture. Although "the impact on the Court of Cassation of some doctrinal writers has been striking", Tunc notes, "relationships between judges and authors are not as fruitful as they could be", not least because the brevity of many judicial decisions means that commentators sometimes "have to guess at the justification and scope of the holdings".[29] To some degree, the very brevity of these decisions might actually explain the vitality of the French case note writing tradition: a tersely expressed opinion, after all, is often an ambiguous opinion, offering considerable leeway for interpretation. It is because French judicial decisions tend to be so brief, furthermore, that the *arrêtistes* can legitimately take it upon themselves to guide the reader of any particular decision through the relevant case law, this being a task which, in Anglo-American law, would normally be performed by the court. As Goutal has commented:

> " 'doctrine' . . . corresponds in France to that active, lively, part of legal scholarship which expresses itself in lengthy notes at the foot of those curt judgments and in articles in legal periodicals . . . The influence . . . of the notes . . . on the development of case-law is dramatic, leading academics to do in France what judges do in England, and the patterns of reasoning and length are not without resemblance; the French 'notes' are much more akin to English judgments than French judgments are . . . [T]his system leaves most of the task of commenting, construing and constructing to law professors. Hence, their influential position".[30]

David observed as far back as the 1940s that the style of judicial discourse and deliberation characteristic of the English system is, in so far is it is replicated within the French tradition, very much the province of the case note writer.[31] It is worth noting also that since the *note d'arrêt* will quite often be based on informal discussions between the *arrêtiste* and the court, it may provide valuable information as well as

[27] Carbonnier, *supra* n. 22, p.138.

[28] See John Bell, Sophie Boyron and Simon Whittaker, *Principles of French Law* (Oxford, Oxford University Press, 1998), pp.35–6.

[29] André Tunc, "Methodology of the Civil Law in France" (1976) 50 *Tulane L. Rev.* 459 at 472. See also Carbonnier, *supra* n. 22, p.138.

[30] Goutal, *supra* n. 3, pp.64–5.

[31] David, *supra* n. 5, pp.140–1.

commentary. Indeed, as Deguergue remarks, the *arrêtiste* may sometimes serve as an "*auxiliare du juge*".[32]

We should note also in this context that, each year, the Cour de cassation hears a formidable number of cases.[33] Not all of these cases will be reported in the *Bulletin de la Cour de cassation.* Of those cases which do appear in the *Bulletin*, the matter of whether they are also to appear in one of the general journals will depend either on a journal editor successfully commissioning a case note or an author offering to write such a note. Either way, the level of visibility of, and the significance accorded to, any decision of the Cour de cassation will to a large extent depend on whether or not that decision has occasioned a *note d'arrêt.*

CASE NOTES AND INFLUENCE

At the beginning of the twenty-first century, case note writing in France appears to be more significant a form of legal commentary than it has ever been. There are at least two reasons for this. During the latter half of the last century, first of all, the French case note evolved into a more ambitious form of legal literature. Whereas traditionally "the case note had been confined to discussion of the decision", Malaurie observed in 1980, "[t]oday, the case commentary is often a note in name only, being a dissertation upon this or that point of law (*Droit*)".[34] (In England, a similar transformation occurred, though only during the 1990s, within

[32] See, generally, Maryse Deguergue, *Jurisprudence et doctrine dans l'élaboration du droit de la responsabilité administrative* (Paris, L.G.D.J., 1994), pp.739–46. Deguergue's remark is perhaps in need of elaboration given that judges in the French administrative law courts (*juges administratifs*) do not normally refer to academic commentary. In the administrative law courts, such commentary is likely to be relied upon by the *Commissaire du Gouvernement*. The *Commissaire du Gouvernement*, contrary to what his title suggests, does not represent the government but is responsible for offering an objective opinion or *conclusion* on the case before the court. The *conclusions* of the *Commissaire du Gouvernement* are invariably carefully researched and will quite often be published in legal journals. Thus, Deguergue's remark that the *arrêtiste* sometimes serves as an "*auxiliare du juge*" might best be interpreted, certainly in relation to administrative law judgments, to mean that *juges administratifs* may be influenced by the scholarly *conclusions* of the *Commissaire du Gouvernement*. Indeed, according to Bell *et al.*, *supra* n. 28, p.58, "the position taken by the *conclusions* will influence the decisions of the judges and it is always advisable to read the decisions of the Conseil d'Etat, in the light of the arguments submitted to it by the *Commissaire du Gouvernement*".

[33] See Bell *et al.*, *supra* n. 28, p.48.

[34] Malaurie, *supra* n. 6, p.88.

the case notes section of the *Modern Law Review*.)[35] Secondly, judicial regard for the pronouncements of *les arrêtistes*—indeed, for legal scholarship generally—has become ever more apparent. It was noted at the outset of this chapter that the higher courts in France have traditionally avoided explicit acknowledgement of legal scholarship.[36] Yet this is a tradition which is possibly heading in the same direction as that comparable, but now extinct, English convention which required judges and counsel to avoid citing as authority the works of living authors (see Chapter 5). In recent years, certain American comparative lawyers have suggested that the relationship between academic and judicial output in France has, in comparison with the relationship which exists in the USA, become strikingly close. "By American standards", Lasser claims, French courts "pay remarkable attention to the opinions expressed by academics and legal commentators. The importance of academic scholarship to the analysis produced by *magistrats* is evidenced by the citation of numerous articles in support of a given proposition".[37] Academic commentary in general, he concludes, "serves an extremely important function in the construction of the legal analysis of the advocate general and the reporting judge".[38]

Why has the tradition of case note writing in France been so venerated and influential? In England the case note is commonly considered to be one of the lowliest forms of legal literature, not least because the case notes section of the law journal often provides a nursery slope for

[35] Throughout the twentieth century, one sees case notes lengthen in the other two long-standing major English law journals, the *Law Quarterly Review*, which was established in 1885, and the *Cambridge Law Journal*, which was established in 1923 but only three volumes of which appeared up until 1932 (whereupon, under the editorship of P. H. Winfield, the journal found its feet). However, only in the *Modern Law Review*, and only in that journal during the 1990s, was the expansion particularly dramatic. The case notes editor of the *Modern Law Review* throughout that decade observes that the watershed note with regard to length was David Miers's piece on the landmark decision of the House of Lords in *Pepper* v. *Hart* [1992] 3 WLR 1032 (see Miers (1993) 56 *M.L.R.* 695), after which the journal began regularly to publish lengthy, generally discursive (as opposed to case-specific) notes: Roger Brownsword, letter to author, 26 May 1999.

[36] We perhaps ought to note that, in France, citations to legal scholarship very occasionally appear in the judgments of lower courts: see Hein Kötz, "Scholarship and the Courts: A Comparative Survey", in D. S. Clark (ed.), *Comparative and Private International Law: Essays in Honor of John Henry Merryman on his Seventieth Birthday* (Berlin, Duncker & Humblot, 1990), pp. 183–95 at 185.

[37] Mitchel de S.-O.-l'E. Lasser, "Judicial (Self-) Portraits: Judicial Discourse in the French Legal System" (1995) 104 *Yale L. J.* 1325 at 1374. In support of the last sentence of this quotation, Lasser cites various *rapports* and *conclusions* of the Cour de cassation dating back to the late 1960s. In much the same comparativist vein, see also Wells, *supra* n. 3, pp.114–15.

[38] Lasser, *supra* n. 37, pp.1375–6.

the tyro academic who has yet to find either the time or the confidence to engage in more sustained research. In the USA, the case commentaries, frequently article-length by English standards, which appear in certain of the law school journals are invariably written by student editors. Most American law professors would consider the writing of such commentaries to be rather beneath them.[39] Why then, in France, has the case note been elevated so?

There are at least four possible answers to this question. First of all, case note writing is a valuable marketing strategy for those French academics who seek to supplement their salaries by acting as *consultants* on behalf of *avocats*. The writer of a case note will very often possess specialist knowledge, having written his or her thesis on the specific branch of law with which the note deals. The case note thus provides the academic with a means of demonstrating his or her expertise to those within the profession who may wish to rely on it. Secondly, French case note writers are rarely legal novices. Case note writing tends to be a task of privilege, a mark of distinction.[40] Part of the reason for this—and this is our third answer—is that French case notes are highly visible. In 1929, an editorial in the *Solicitors' Journal* praised the editor of the *Dominion Law Reports* for adopting the convention of including notes in each issue on the most important cases. "Although somewhat novel", the editorial opined, "there is much to be said in favour of the plan adopted by our Canadian confrères".[41] While the *All England Law Reports* carried editorial notes in its earliest volumes (1936–1940), and while certain specialist journals combine case reporting and case commentary,[42] the dominant English convention has been to publish case law and case notes in separate fora. As intimated in the discussion above, however, the French tend to publish their case notes in the case reports, under-

[39] Of course, a rather different type of case commentary, one which I except from my assertion here, is the *Harvard Law Review* "Foreword". Having appeared in the journal since 1951, the Harvard Foreword is a survey of the work of the Supreme Court, undertaken each year by one or another prominent scholar of constitutional law. Within the American academic-legal system, to be accorded the opportunity to write a Harvard Foreword is clearly an indication of high esteem. See generally Mark Tushnet and Timothy Lynch, "The Project of the Harvard *Forewords*: A Social and Intellectual Inquiry" (1994–95) 11 *Constitutional Commentary* 463.

[40] See Max Radin, "Sources of Law—New and Old" (1928) 1 *Southern Calif. L. Rev.* 411 at 419.

[41] Anon., "Law Reports with Editorial Comments" (1929) 73 *Sol. Jo.* 241.

[42] The *Family Law Journal*, for example, contains summaries of and (often influential) academic commentaries on cases reported at length in the *Family Law Reports*. The *Criminal Law Review* also provides summaries of and commentaries on cases. (We will discuss this last example in Chapter 5.)

neath the relevant decisions.[43] It is interesting to note Max Radin's comment from the 1920s, even if it probably is something of an overstatement, that "[o]ne of the three collections of French reports, the *Dalloz*, the *Sirey*, or the *Gazette du Palais*, is read by almost every lawyer in France and the brief decision would be unintelligible and useless to him without the notes which are attached to them".[44] The juxtapositioning of cases and case notes not only means that the latter are more likely to be read by legal practitioners and judges but also that the most incisive notes are unlikely to go unappreciated, for the notes appear as immediate responses to the outcome and so lend themselves to easy comparison with the actual judgments.[45] Case notes thus provide legal commentators with the opportunity to operate as shadow-judges, to showcase their doctrinal skills and to try to influence judicial thinking in the future. It hardly seems surprising that the distinguished academic lawyer should normally revel in the role of *l'arrêtiste*.

The fourth answer to the question which we have posed relates to the professional status of this distinguished academic lawyer. Historically, as we have already noted, the law faculty and the judiciary in France have enjoyed a fairly close relationship. This relationship remains close to this day.[46] The relevance of the professional status of academic lawyers is not wholly explicable, however, by reference to the fact that the most eminent among them have been able to make their voices heard among the judiciary. We ought also to take note of the inherently elitist nature of the academic legal profession in France. As with the French legal profession generally, the legal academy is markedly hierarchical.[47] Academic background, social status, professional location and

[43] Hence the French style of citing the case note as published underneath the relevant case: e.g., Jacques Ghestin, note D. 1974, 414 sous Cass. com. 12 févr. 1974. See further Wells, *supra* n. 3, p.114; Dawson, *supra* n. 16, p.398; and Tunc, *supra* n. 29, pp.471–2.

[44] Radin, *supra* n. 40, p.419.

[45] The converse of this, of course, is that poorly-executed case notes might look all the worse owing to their positioning. Indeed given the high visibility of case notes, and the fact that a poorly-conceived note might cause considerable embarrassment and annoyance, it seems likely that case note editors will take a fairly conservative approach to commissioning.

[46] See Pierre Bourdieu, "The Force of Law: Toward a Sociology of the Juridical Field" (1987) 38 *Hastings L. J.* 805 at 822–5 (Eng. trans. R. Terdiman).

[47] See Jean Rivero, "La formation et le recrutement des professeurs des Facultés de Droit françaises" (1962) 59 *Doctrina: Revista de derecho, jurisprudencia y administración* (Uruguay) 249 (Rivero's article appears here in both Spanish and French). On hierarchy within the French legal profession more generally, see Lucien Karpik, *French Lawyers: A Study in Collective Action, 1274 to 1994* (Eng. trans. N. Scott, Oxford, Clarendon Press, 1999), pp.191–206.

the ability to secure publication in the most eminent periodicals are all indicative of whether or not one belongs to the élite.[48] This in itself hardly distinguishes French legal academics from their colleagues in many other jurisdictions. It is also the case in France, however, that those within the élite are generally held in high regard as legal experts and lawyer-statesmen. Writing in the 1980s, Bourdieu noted "the role of consultant to governments and international bodies played by jurists, notably by specialists in international law, commercial law or public law" and claimed that, in France, "law professors . . . are more likely than science or arts professors to combine functions of authority in the university with positions of power in the political world or even in the business world".[49] A considerable number of French law professors have enjoyed distinguished careers as government ministers, and some have been appointed to the Cour de cassation.[50] "Some are also advisers in the *conseil d'état*, where the drafting of statutes is performed or controlled, and thus influence legislation in a direct way."[51] French legal culture is by no means indifferent to academic lawyers and their viewpoints.

That successful French legal academics are often respected and sought out for their expertise and judgments makes them somewhat similar to their North American counterparts. We have seen, however, that many American law professors produce scholarship which judges do not find particularly useful. Legal commentary in France, by contrast, tends to be less abstruse and more pertinent to judicial concerns. In particular, the value that French lawyers place on the pithy, analytical *note d'arrêt* which appears alongside the case report means that the legal academy is predominantly responsible for the production of a body of legal literature which judges generally read and respect. As Troper and Grzegorczyk observe, the influence of such literature on the courts tends not to be "direct and immediately operating. Rather it is a 'long-term' trend representing the progressive penetration of the most

[48] See Philippe Jestaz and Christophe Jamin, "The Entity of French Doctrine: Some Thoughts on the Community of French Writers" (1998) 18 *Legal Studies* 415 at 430–3.

[49] Pierre Bourdieu, *Homo Academicus* (Eng. trans. P. Collier, Cambridge, Polity Press, 1988 [1984]), pp.51–2.

[50] On ministerial careers, see Bell *et al.*, *supra* n. 28, p.36; Jestaz and Jamin, *supra* n. 48, p.420. On elevation of law professors to the Cour de cassation, see Jestaz and Jamin, *ibid.*, p.423; and Tunc, *supra* n. 29, p.471.

[51] R. C. van Caenegem, *Judges, Legislators and Professors: Chapters in European Legal History* (Cambridge, Cambridge University Press, 1987), p.87.

influential ideas and dogmatic constructions in judicial practice".[52] It is worth noting also that our account of the French scene shows how citation does not necessarily capture the notion of influence. Although the increasing tendency of modern French judges to cite commentators highlights the important advisory role played by academics, this role is not in itself new. Increased citation of academics by judges draws attention to the influence of doctrinal writing on French judicial thought, but such writing has been influential at least since the mid-nineteenth century.

In very crude terms, the relationship between academics and courts in England falls somewhere between the American and the French experiences. English academic lawyers, as with their American and unlike their French counterparts, have dealt with a judiciary which has placed a premium on discursiveness and reasoning. As with their French and unlike their American counterparts, however, the English courts have traditionally been reluctant explicitly to acknowledge much in the way of juristic influence. Yet, as with France so too with England: the lack of explicit acknowledgement does not necessitate the conclusion that academics have been uninfluential.

[52] Michel Troper and Christophe Grzegorczyk, "Precedent in France", in D. Neil MacCormick and Robert S. Summers (eds), *Interpreting Precedents: A Comparative Study* (Dartmouth, Ashgate, 1997), pp.103–10 at 123.

5

England

WHEREAS AMERICAN LAW reviews tend to follow strict rules about citation style, their English equivalents are less interested in the subject. Not only do the English lack a uniform system of citation (most law periodicals produce brief and idiosyncratic guides for contributors) but it is also possible to find within as well as among the journals significant variations in citation form. This relaxed approach to citation convention is not necessarily a bad thing.[1] The important point to note for our purposes is that the difference between the Americans and the English over citation concerns not just style but also the significance of the activity. Not for the English the citation surveys, the lists of most-cited legal articles and the journal issues dedicated to legal citations and their relevance. The English, in short, do not place as much store in citations as do the Americans.

Or rather, as compared with their American counterparts, English academic lawyers do not accord as much significance to citations to one another. When the citation is to be found not in the work of an academic but in the opinion of a judge, its value seems to multiply. In the late 1980s, a lecturer in the Law Department at the London School of Economics reported that the House of Lords' citation of an article written by one of his colleagues prompted a circular from the head of department drawing attention to the matter.[2] In England, legal academics expect to be cited by other legal academics. But they rarely expect to be cited by judges. Even though the English courts are nowadays generally more inclined to cite academic commentary, such practice is by no means routine.

[1] See Pierre Legrand, *Fragments on Law-as-Culture* (Deventer, Tjeenk Willink, 1999), pp.43–5.

[2] See W. T. Murphy, Book Review [1987] *Public Law* 640. The citation in question was by Lord Goff in *Spiliada Maritime Corp*. v. *Cansulex Ltd*. [1987] 1 AC 460, 488 (citing, *inter alios*, Schuz).

THE VALUE OF DEATH

Why should English academic lawyers consider judicial acknowledgement of their work to be noteworthy? Perhaps the answer is that the value of such work is something which the judiciary has often appeared determined not to acknowledge. Although we will discover that the image of an English judiciary generally blinkered to academic initiative is rather misleading, it is not surprising that the image should have evolved and persisted. It seems highly unlikely, indeed would be near-ludicrous to suggest, that English judges endeavoured in the past to develop a strategy for demoralizing legal academics. Yet that nebulous convention against the citation of living authors in English courts could hardly have been better designed to undermine the status and self-confidence of the academic lawyer.[3]

It seems inappropriate to refer to a distinct *rule* against the citation of living authors in court, since nothing more than a convention appears ever to have existed.[4] In *Ion's Case* (1852), counsel claimed—and the presiding judges did not dispute—that there "is no doubt a rule that a writer on law is not to be considered an authority in his lifetime".[5] Yet the footnote to this remark elaborates that "[t]his rule

[3] Not that the convention was always formulated specifically in relation to academic writings. Sometimes, judges would suggest that courts ought only to consider textbooks prepared by members of the Bar. In *Re Thompson* [1936] Ch. 676, after counsel for the trustees had cited the sixth edition of Dymond on *Estate Duties*, Clauson J. asked: "Can I look at this book? I thought the practice of the Court was to look only at text-books prepared by members of the Bar, which this book is not" (*ibid.* 680). The judge passed no comment when, during the same proceedings, counsel for the legatee cited, *inter alia,* the 21st edition of Snell's *Equity* (this edition having been prepared by a solicitor): see *ibid.* 679. On another occasion, a former Master of the Rolls singled out textbooks by barristers as being not suitable for consideration in court: see *Tichborne* v. *Weir* (1892) 67 LT 735, 736, per Lord Esher, MR ("Text-books written by living authors who are practising barristers are not quoted in the courts").

[4] Dawson, writing in the late-1960s, refers to it as a "rule of judicial etiquette" which "is being gradually relaxed". John P. Dawson, *The Oracles of the Law* (Ann Arbor, University of Michigan Law School, 1968), p.97. Other commentators have looked upon the convention similarly: see, e.g., D. L. Carey Miller, "Legal Writings as a Source in English Law" (1975) 8 *Compar. & Int'l. L. J. of Southern Africa* 236 at 240; Hein Kötz, "Scholarship and the Courts: A Comparative Survey", in D. S. Clark (ed.), *Comparative and Private International Law: Essays in Honor of John Henry Merryman on his Seventieth Birthday* (Berlin, Duncker & Humblot, 1990), pp.183–95 at 187–90; and Peter Birks, "Adjudication and Interpretation in the Common Law: A Century of Change" (1994) 14 *Legal Studies* 156 at 163.

[5] *R.* v. *Ion* (1852) 2 Den. CC 475, 488; 169 Eng. Rep. 588, 594.

seems 'more honoured in the breach than in the observance' ".[6] Kekewich J. endeavoured to reinforce the "rule" in 1887 when, having observed that counsel's argument in the case before him had "almost entirely rested upon one passage in the work of Lord Justice *Fry* on Specific Performance", he commented that:

> "It is to my mind much to be regretted, and it is a regret which I believe every Judge on the bench shares, that text-books are more and more quoted in Court—I mean of course text-books by living authors—and some Judges have gone so far as to say that they shall not be quoted".[7]

Note that Kekewich was trying to defy the tide: he re-stated the rule because barristers were ever more persistently breaking it. Note also that blame for the breach was being laid at the feet of barristers rather than judges.[8] Even Lord Justice Fry himself, Kekewich claimed, cautioned against the citation of living authors in court.[9] The notion that "works written or revised by authors on the Bench . . . possess a quasi-judicial authority", Fry contended, "seems . . . in part at least erroneous" since it neglects "how different are the circumstances under which a book is written and a judgment pronounced".[10] There is a

[6] *Ibid.*, p.594 n. *b*. See further Percy H. Winfield, *The Chief Sources of English Legal History* (Cambridge, Mass., Harvard University Press, 1925), pp.255–6. In the eighteenth century there was adopted with similar inconsistency a convention against the citation of civilian literature before the English courts: see, e.g., *Omychund* v. *Barker* (1744) 1 Atk. 21, 37; 26 Eng. Rep. 15, 25; not that this convention prevented civilian literature from influencing the development of the common law. For illustrations of such influence, see J. W. Tubbs, *The Common Law Mind: Medieval and Early Modern Conceptions* (Baltimore, Johns Hopkins University Press, 2000), pp.26–8 (on pre-eighteenth century influences); A. W. B. Simpson, "Innovation in Nineteenth Century Contract Law" (1975) 91 *L.Q.R.* 247; and David Ibbetson, "'The Law of Business Rome': Foundations of the Anglo-American Tort of Negligence" (1999) 52 *Current Legal Problems* 74.

[7] *Union Bank* v. *Munster* (1887) 37 Ch D. 51, 54.

[8] Writing in the late 1940s, David argued (but provided scant support for the proposition) that although judges forbade counsel from citing living authors in court, they took a rather more relaxed approach to the convention when applying it to themselves. See René David, *Introduction à l'étude du droit privé de l'Angleterre* (Paris, Recueil Sirey, 1948), pp.168–9.

[9] See *Union Bank* v. *Munster*, *supra* n. 7, at 54 ("In the preface to this very book we have a warning against it by the learned author himself").

[10] Sir Edward Fry, *A Treatise on the Specific Performance of Contracts*, (2nd edn., London, Stevens, 1881), p.vii. The passage is omitted from later editions. It might be noted also that the passage is taken from the Preface of the book, and that Fry's prefatory remarks tended, in keeping with the dominant style of this period, to be modest and self-deprecating. Hence, in the Preface to the first edition he claims to "offer this little book to the members of my profession . . . with . . . diffidence, because I am not ignorant of the difficulties of the subject on which I have written, or of the shortcomings of my own performance": Sir Edward Fry, *A Treatise on the Specific Performance of Contracts:*

degree of irony in the fact that, in supporting the so-called rule against citation, Kekewich himself sidestepped it: he "cannot forbear from quoting the words" of Fry.[11] More pertinently, Fry's own contention was not that living authors should never be cited in court but, as Birks observes, "that law books cannot be safely relied upon . . . to do the same work which is normally done by cases".[12] Perhaps most remarkably of all, not only was it not unheard of for judges of this era to endorse the citation of living authors in court,[13] but, little more than two months before *Union Bank* v. *Munster* was decided, Kekewich himself had breached the convention.[14] Indeed, prior to the *Union Bank* decision "he had allowed textbooks to be cited in his court with considerable frequency".[15]

Other judicial efforts to support the convention against citation seem no less questionable than that made by Kekewich. "I think we ought in this Court still to maintain the old idea", Lord Justice Vaughan Williams remarked in 1913, "that counsel are not entitled to quote living authors as authorities for a proposition they are putting forward, but they may adopt the author's statements as part of their argument".[16] Buried within this passage is an acknowledgement which Kekewich had rendered explicit: that not everyone was adhering to the convention against citation. We ought to maintain the convention, Vaughan Williams appears to be arguing, notwithstanding the fact that there is evidence of a movement away from it. His formulation of this

Including those of Public Companies, with a Preliminary Chapter on the Provisions of the Chancery Amendment Act (London, Butterworths, 1858), p.iii. (The first edition was over 450 pages in length.)

[11] *Union Bank* v. *Munster*, *supra* n. 7, at 54.

[12] Birks, *supra* n. 4, p.164.

[13] Twelve years after the decision in *Union Bank* v. *Munster*, Byrne J, citing a variety of commentaries (including *Fry on Specific Performance*), declared that "[f]or the exposition of our very complicated real property law, it is proper in the absence of judicial authority to resort to text-books which have been recognised by the Courts as representing the views and practice of conveyancers of repute": *Re Hollis' Hospital and Hague's Contract* [1899] 2 Ch. 540, 551, 555.

[14] *Foster* v. *Wheeler* (1887) 36 Ch. D 695, 698 (Kekewich J favourably citing the third edition of *Pollock on Contracts*). *Foster* v. *Wheeler* was decided on 12 August 1887, whereas *Union Bank* v. *Munster* was decided 31 October 1887.

[15] David Pugsley, "London Tramways (1898)" (1996) 17 *Jnl. Leg. Hist.* 172 at 174. How might we explain Kekewich's change of attitude? Pugsley suggests that Kekewich was very much under the influence of the then Lord Chancellor, Lord Halsbury, and that during the long vacation of 1887 Halsbury (who, having crossed swords with Pollock, probably preferred not to see him cited in court) had most likely had a word in Kekewich's ear.

[16] *Greenlands* v. *Wilmhurst* (1913) 29 TLR 685, 687 (CA).

argument is especially striking because it separates influence and citation: while it is acceptable for counsel to be influenced by living commentators, it is inappropriate for them to acknowledge that influence. It is difficult to interpret this viewpoint as anything other than judicial endorsement of a practice which in academic circles would be regarded as plagiarism.

A more palatable expression of the viewpoint was offered by Lord Buckmaster in *Donoghue* v. *Stevenson* (1932), when he proclaimed that "the work of living authors, however deservedly eminent, cannot be used as authority, though the opinions they express may demand attention".[17] Four years later, and possibly prompted by Buckmaster's words, Lord Wright in *Nicholls* v. *Ely Beet Sugar Factory* relied upon and mischievously referred to the thirteenth edition of the then nonagenarian Sir Frederick Pollock's *The Law of Torts* as "fortunately not a work of authority".[18] We will see in due course that there were, by this point in time, plenty of other indications in the law reports that a significant number of judges paid little if any attention to the convention against citation.

It ought to be emphasized, nevertheless, that while explicit judicial support for the convention may have been diminishing by the middle of the twentieth century, many, indeed most, judges continued to adhere to it.[19] "In the 1950s", Paterson has claimed, "barristers by and large seem to have felt unable to breach the non-citation rule in arguments before the Lords".[20] Recalling his days as a law student in the early 1960s, Birks has remarked that "we still took in the message that it was only exceptionally that a living author might be cited in court,

[17] *Donoghue* v. *Stevenson* [1932] AC 562, 567 (HL). The statement seems almost ironic, given that Lord Atkin's speech in this case has often been assumed to owe something to the views of Percy Winfield (d. 1953). See *Donoghue* v. *Stevenson* at 578–9, 599 (per Lord Atkin); and cf. Percy H. Winfield, "The History of Negligence in the Law of Torts" (1926) 42 *L.Q.R.* 184 at 196.

[18] *Nicholls* v. *Ely Beet Sugar Factory Ltd.* [1936] Ch. 343, 349 (CA). After quoting from *The Law of Torts*, Wright adds: "[t]he words apply exactly to the present case, and I accept them as part of my judgment". In two sets of law reports, Wright was misquoted as saying "unfortunately" rather than "fortunately". See R. E. Megarry, *Miscellany-at-Law: A Diversion for Lawyers and Others* (London, Stevens, 1955), p.328. Pollock died on 18 January 1937, aged 91. That Wright held Pollock in high regard is evident from, among other things, the fact that he wrote two obituaries of the man: see (1937) 53 *L.Q.R.* 151; *D.N.B. (1931–1940)*, pp.711–13.

[19] See Lord Diplock, "A. L. G.: A Judge's View" (1975) 91 *L.Q.R.* 457 at 458 ("It seems scarcely credible today that the rule against citation from the works of living academic writers persisted until after the Second World War").

[20] Alan Paterson, *The Law Lords* (London, Macmillan, 1982), p.16.

something which I accepted without question as part of the natural order".[21] Echoing Lord Justice Vaughan Williams, Hood Phillips wrote in 1970 that while textbooks may be "looked at by judges and practitioners . . . for the purpose of acquiring personal information and ideas for argument, and for finding references to statutes and reported cases", the "general rule" remains "that textbooks . . . however eminent their authors, are not treated as authorities".[22] Even as late as 1980, by which point appeal court judgments containing references to living authors were regularly being handed down,[23] it is possible to find concern being expressed in the House of Lords over "the dangers, well perceived by our predecessors but tending to be neglected in modern times, of placing reliance on textbook authority for an analysis of judicial decisions".[24]

More interesting than the convention against citation itself are the reasons which might be offered in support of it. At least eight possible reasons might be identified. First, the growth of law reporting after Blackstone's era and the resulting accessible store of common law principles ensured that it was no longer necessary to rely on textbooks for second-hand renderings of cases.[25] Secondly, the declaratory theory of law—a theory which was subscribed to by many English judges certainly until the mid-twentieth century—seemed to preclude the possibility of treating textbooks as legal authorities. Austin disparaged this theory as "the childish fiction employed by our judges, that judiciary or common law is not made by them, but is a miraculous something made by nobody, existing, I suppose, from eternity and merely *declared* from time to time by the judges".[26] As if endeavouring to play into Austin's hands, Lord Esher in 1892 proclaimed that:

[21] Birks, *supra* n. 4, p.165.

[22] O. Hood Phillips, *A First Book of English Law*, (6th edn., London, Sweet & Maxwell, 1970), p.222.

[23] See Carey Miller, *supra* n. 4, pp.240, 242–4; and Peter Birks, "The Academic and the Practitioner" (1998) 18 *Legal Studies* 397 at 398.

[24] *Johnson* v. *Agnew* [1980] AC 367, 395 (per Lord Wilberforce); and see further Paterson, *supra* n. 20, pp.17–19; but cf. Lord Wilberforce, "La Chambre des Lords" (1978) 30 *Rev. Int. Droit Comparé* 85 at 95 where it is noted that "[t]he notes of certain commentators . . . have exerted a considerable influence" and where especial tribute is paid to Arthur Goodhart's ability to influence judicial decision-making primarily through his case notes in the *Law Quarterly Review* (of which Goodhart was at this time editor). For further discussion of Goodhart, see below.

[25] See Blackstone, *Commentaries on the Laws of England*, Intro., iii, 72–3; also Carey Miller, *supra* n. 4, p.239.

[26] John Austin, *Lectures on Jurisprudence, or the Philosophy of Positive Law*, 2 vols. (R. Campbell (ed.), 5th edn., London, John Murray, 1885), II, p.634.

"[t]here is in fact no such thing as judge-made law, for the judges do not make the law, though they frequently have to apply existing law to circumstances as to which it has not previously been authoritatively laid down that such law is applicable".[27]

The shortcomings of the declaratory theory have been thoroughly explored elsewhere and do not concern us here.[28] More important for our purposes is the fact that acceptance of the theory appears to mean treating all extra-judicial opinion as unauthoritative. For anyone who accepts the declaratory theory, the occasions on which any academic commentary might appropriately be cited in court are rare, since the jurist is little if anything more than a helpful expositor of the law.

A third possible reason for the convention against the citation of living authors is the fear of causing offence. A judge might oppose citation of the work of living jurist A in court out of a concern that such citation may offend other living jurists who consider their own opinions to be just as authoritative and relevant as those of A. Judges reduce opportunities for juristic *Sturm und Drang* where they condone the citation only of those commentators who are no longer alive: those who see their work passed over in silence can console themselves, after all, with the thought that they might have been treated differently were they dead.[29] Fourthly, the convention may have been favoured in order to prevent or reduce judicial citation of immature or unreflective commentary. "[T]he passage of years and the activities of those who edit the books of the departed", Megarry has argued, "tend to produce criticism and sometimes the elimination of frailties, and so give greater confidence in what remains".[30] A fifth reason for the convention is that

[27] *Willis* v. *Baddeley* [1892] 2 QB 324, 326 (CA). For proclamations in much the same vein, see also *Baylis* v. *Bishop of London* [1913] 1 Ch. 127, 137 (per Farwell LJ); *Harnett* v. *Fisher* [1927] 1 KB 402, 424 (per Scrutton LJ); and also the illustrations to be found in Tom Bingham, *The Business of Judging: Selected Essays and Speeches* (Oxford, Oxford University Press, 2000), pp.25–7.

[28] For what is probably still the best exploration of the shortcomings see John Chipman Gray, *The Nature and Sources of the Law* (2nd. edn., New York, Macmillan, 1921), pp.93–103, 219–33. For a judicial critique of the theory see Bingham, *supra* n. 27, pp.28–30.

[29] Honoré has speculated that it is this fear of causing offence which probably explains why jurists of the late Roman classical period were disinclined to cite contemporaries while they were alive. "They may have been sensitive to the danger of giving or receiving offence, or *iniuria*. It is easier and safer to express one's real opinion of a dead author": Tony Honoré, *Ulpian* (Oxford, Clarendon Press, 1982), p.218.

[30] Megarry, *supra* n. 18, p.328. Megarry offers another reason: "there are a number of living authors whose appearance and demeanour do something to sap any confidence in their omniscience which the printed page may have instilled; the dead, on the other hand,

whereas the American style of judicial opinion-writing is conducive to inordinate citation, the English style pushes in the other direction.[31] English appellate decisions, as Lawson has observed, tend to be:

> "delivered orally from the Bench immediately after the close of oral argument or after a very short interval . . . The judges . . . do not go home to do extensive research and they have no one to help them like the American law clerks . . . Judgment will be reserved in order to give the judges time for consideration, and no doubt the written judgment will usually be a more finished product. But it will be on the same general lines as an oral judgment".[32]

An American judge, after watching the presentation of arguments in the Court of Appeal during October 1995, remarked in relation to one particular case that:

> "The barrister argued for about half an hour . . . At the conclusion the judges retired for no more than five minutes, then returned to the bench, and the presiding judge, speaking without pauses, dictated an opinion . . . A transcript of the oral opinion was submitted to the judge, who made minute corrections, limited almost entirely to punctuation . . . When one considers that the judges' exposure to the case consisted essentially of a half hour argument by a barrister with no briefs, no adversary presentation, no assistance from law clerks, and no time for extended reflection, the performance of the presiding judge in extemporizing [an] elegant and comprehensive opinion is remarkable by American standards".[33]

Being essentially an oral tradition, the English adjudicative process "is not conducive to the more ample citation practices found in some civil law countries and in the United States".[34] Although the incorporation of citations to academic literature into judgments delivered from the bench is obviously not impossible, and although it is easy—leaving

so often leave little clue to what manner of men they were save the majestic skill with which they have arrayed the learning of centuries and exposed the failings of the bench": *ibid.*

[31] For a critique of the American style, by an American judge, for its tendency to encourage excessive citation, see Abner J. Mikva, "Goodbye to Footnotes" (1985) 56 *Univ. Colorado L. Rev.* 647.

[32] F. H. Lawson, "Comparative Judicial Style" (1977) 25 *Am. J. Compar. Law* 364 at 364–6.

[33] Richard A. Posner, *Law and Legal Theory in England and America* (Oxford, Clarendon Press, 1996), p.126. While Posner is no doubt right to draw attention to this talent for extemporization, it ought to be noted that the Court of Appeal would have known before the hearing the point of law at issue. See further Lord Mustill, "What do Judges do?" [1995–96] no. 3 *Juridisk Tidskrift* 611 at 621.

[34] Kötz, *supra* n. 4, p.189.

aside the matter of whether it is considered acceptable—for counsel to refer informally to such literature in their arguments, an oral adjudicative culture is, as compared with an equivalent culture of writing, likely to accommodate, rely upon and encourage citation to a lesser extent.[35]

A sixth possible reason for the convention concerns not so much how judges see academics but how academics have sometimes regarded themselves. The environment of the modern English academic lawyer is highly competitive. Recruitment and promotion depends primarily on one's achievements and ambition as a researcher. Today, those who do not publish—whether through lack of drive, talent or confidence—are unlikely to survive in this environment, assuming they can secure an appointment in the first place. But it was not always thus. In the early 1970s, in an interview with a national newspaper, one Oxford law don was reported as being both dismissive of and too busy to undertake research.[36] While it would be irresponsible to read too much into an isolated statement of this nature, other observations from the period reinforce the basic message. Developing the thesis that the fundamental purpose of the university is to cultivate the life of the mind, Annan had argued a decade earlier that the retention of law—"which (as taught in England) is the most flagrantly vocational of all traditional subjects"—on the academic syllabus "remain[s] mysterious".[37] "If academic lawyers are being honest", Bridge wrote in 1975, "they will admit that there is still too little legal research being done".[38] Although legal academics "have certainly progressed from being mere technicians", he concluded, they "still do not advance their subject to the same degree as other academics advance theirs".[39]

History attests to this image of the academic lawyer as underachiever. "[T]he law school", wrote Winstanley in his *Early Victorian Cambridge*, "was generally recognised to be a refuge for those who were averse to intellectual effort".[40] The first chair of law in England,

[35] See Walter J. Ong, *Orality and Literacy: The Technologizing of the Word* (London, Methuen, 1982), p.34.

[36] Jilly Cooper, "A Bird for High Table", *Sunday Times*, 14 January 1973, pp.25–26 at 25 (quoting an Oxford law don as saying that "I'm really too busy to do any research. After all . . . what is research but copying down what other people have written with varying degrees of accuracy?").

[37] Noel Annan, "The Universities" (1963) 20(4) *Encounter* 3 at 10.

[38] J. W. Bridge, "The Academic Lawyer: Mere Working Mason or Architect?" (1975) 91 *L.Q.R.* 488 at 494.

[39] *Ibid.*, p.501.

[40] D. A. Winstanley, *Early Victorian Cambridge* (Cambridge, Cambridge University Press, 1940), p.3.

the Vinerian chair, was not established until 1758: before Blackstone's appointment to that post "there had never been, anywhere, a professor of the common law".[41] When, three-quarters of a century later, a chair of English law was established at King's College, London, its incumbent revealed that members of the legal profession had urged him to decline the post on the basis that "the office of a Law Professor was undesirable for a practising lawyer; for any one, in short, but those who had nothing else to do".[42] Although there had been established in the 1870s faculties of law at Oxford and Cambridge, Dicey noted in his inaugural lecture at the former institution in 1883 that "the non-existence till recent years of any legal professoriate" had ensured that there existed "no history of English law as a whole deserving of the name".[43] In his inaugural lecture at Cambridge during the same year, Pollock sounded an even gloomier note: "the scientific and systematic study of law", he lamented, is "a pursuit still followed in this land by few, scorned or depreciated by many".[44] Of course, the few who were following that pursuit—figures such as Anson, Bryce, Maine and Maitland (along, of course, with Dicey and Pollock themselves)—are now remembered as among the great English jurists. They constituted, however, a generation with few successors.[45] "We have accomplished less than we hoped", Bryce wrote in his valedictory lecture at Oxford in 1893:

> "in raising up a band of young lawyers who would maintain, even in the midst of London practice, an interest in legal history and juristic speculation. The number of persons in England who care for either subject is undeniably small, probably smaller, in proportion to the size and influence of the

[41] Birks, *supra* n. 23, p.398.

[42] J. J. Park, *The Dogmas of the Constitution: Four Lectures, being the First, Tenth, Eleventh, & Thirteenth, of a Course on the Theory & Practice of the Constitution* (London, B. Fellowes, 1832), p.2; and see also Bridge, *supra* n. 38, p.490.

[43] A. V. Dicey, *Can English Law be Taught at the Universities?* (London, Macmillan & Co., 1883), p.22.

[44] Frederick Pollock, *English Opportunities and Duties in the Historical and Comparative Study of Law* (London, Macmillan & Co., 1883), p.5.

[45] See generally Brian Abel-Smith and Robert Stevens, *Lawyers and the Courts: A Sociological Study of the English Legal System, 1750–1965* (London, Heinemann, 1967), pp.166–8; and also F. H. Lawson, "Doctrinal Writing: A Foreign Element in English Law?", in E. von Caemmerer, S. Menstschikoff and K. Zweigert (eds), *Ius privatum gentium. Festschrift für Max Rheinstein zum 70. Geburtstag am 5. Juli 1969*, 2 vols., (Tübingen, Mohr (Seibeck), 1969), I, pp.191–210 at 200 (noting "a general decline in the quantity and quality of mental activity among lawyers after the brilliant performance of the mid-Victorian age").

profession, than in any other civilized country; and it increases so slowly as to seem to discredit the efforts of the Universities".[46]

Academic law remained a fairly moribund, amateurish profession throughout the first half of the twentieth century. Never mind that judges were disinclined to allow citation of academic writings in court; academics, what few there were, were often disinclined to write. In his Presidential address to the Society of Public Teachers of Law (SPTL) in 1999, Bell observed that neither of the two professors from his own institution who had previously served as SPTL Presidents would have been particularly preoccupied by research. "Neither Professor Phillips (President 1914) nor Professor Hughes (President 1931) wrote anything significant. For them, the subjects on which they wrote were hobbies, as much as fishing at his home in North Wales was for Professor Hughes."[47] "[O]utside one or two posts like the Vinerian professorship", wrote Laski to Holmes in 1929, "the law teachers are a very inferior set of people who mainly teach because they cannot make a success of the bar"[48] and who regard research "as a merely professional by-product instead of being central to the profession and its organisation".[49] The English academic lawyer's tendency towards low self-esteem was noted by Laski four years earlier when, having attended a SPTL dinner, he observed that "the judges who were the guests had, with two exceptions, a most amusing sense of infinite superiority", while the academics exhibited "a sense of complete inferiority".[50]

[46] James Bryce, "Legal Studies in the University of Oxford" (1893), in his *Studies in History and Jurisprudence*, 2 vols. (Oxford, Clarendon Press, 1901), II, pp.504–25 at 518.

[47] John Bell, "Research and the Law Teacher" (2000) 20 *S.P.T.L. Reporter* 5–7 at 5. In his Presidential Address to the SPTL in 1948, W. T. S. Stallybrass began by mixing self-deprecation and candour: "I am afraid that I never was learned and in the last two years have not had time to make myself learned and I have not had time even to write out what I am going to say . . . I am afraid that I may be covering ground covered by older Addresses, though I have not had time to re-read them": W. T. S. Stallybrass, "Law in the Universities" (1948) n.s. 1 *J.S.P.T.L.* 157. Stallybrass then proceeded to speak on the subject of law teaching in the universities, concluding that "there is a tendency to too much specialisation" among university law teachers (*ibid.*, p.165).

[48] Laski to Holmes, 11 June 1929, in M. DeWolfe Howe (ed.), *Holmes-Laski Letters: The Correspondence of Mr. Justice Holmes and Harold J. Laski, 1916–1935*, 2 vols., (London, Geoffrey Cumberlege, 1953), II, p.1156; and cf. Steve Hedley, "Words, Words, Words: Making Sense of Legal Judgments, 1875–1940", in C. Stebbings (ed.), *Law Reporting in Britain: Proceedings of the Eleventh British Legal History Conference* (London, The Hambledon Press, 1995), pp.169–86 at 177.

[49] Laski to Holmes, 21 May 1933, in *Holmes-Laski Letters*, *supra* n. 48, II, p.1441.

[50] Laski to Holmes, 13 July 1925, *ibid.*, I, p.763. In a similar vein, see also Laski to Holmes, 23 July 1932, *ibid.*, II, pp.1398–9. On Laski's unsuccessful efforts to change

Much the same observation is to be found in Gower's inaugural lecture at the London School of Economics twenty-five years later:

> "[N]othing is more nauseating than the patronising air of mock humility usually affected by one of His Majesty's judges when addressing an academic gathering. A psychiatrist will doubtless diagnose from these remarks that I am suffering from an inferiority complex. Precisely. It is my submission that English teachers of law suffer from an acute inferiority complex and that this is a bad thing for the profession as a whole".[51]

The status of law in the universities, and of university lawyers, until this point makes it hardly surprising that academic commentaries were rarely being cited in court. The academic-legal profession, in so far as there was such a profession, simply lacked presence. "By the 1950s", Bridge observes, "there were established law schools in the universities but . . . [t]here was no widely established practice of legal research".[52] Little had changed by the middle of the following decade: "[u]niversity law faculties . . . still lacked prestige with other university faculties and with the profession. In general law departments were small and poorly equipped and had failed to attract a fair share of the best talent in the profession".[53]

Since the 1960s, none the less, the academic-legal profession has been developing rapidly. In 1974, the SPTL had just over 700 teaching members; in 1953 it had just over 200.[54] Today, it has almost 2,500.[55] Perhaps the English courts are nowadays more inclined to permit citations of, and indeed to cite, academic commentary because, like the legal academy itself, such commentary has become so much more of a presence; never before in England have there been so many academic lawyers producing so much specialist literature. Just as few barristers and judges would wish—let alone have the energy—to read all of this literature, one expects that few of them would be happy or even able to

attitudes towards academic law and legal education in England, see Abel-Smith and Stevens, *supra* n. 45, pp.183–5.

[51] L. C. B. Gower, "English Legal Training: A Critical Survey" (1950) 13 *M.L.R.* 137 at 198. In his Presidential Address to the SPTL in 1977, Gower recounted how the Law Lords had summoned to their presence and reproved the then General Editor of the *Modern Law Review*, Lord Chorley, for having published Gower's claim that many judges patronize academics. See L. C. B. Gower, "Looking Back" (1978) n.s. 14 *J.S.P.T.L.* 155; also Cyril Glasser, "Radicals and Refugees: The Foundation of the Modern Law Review and English Legal Scholarship" (1987) 50 *M.L.R.* 688 at 703–5.

[52] Bridge, *supra* n. 38, p.493.

[53] Abel-Smith and Stevens, *supra* n. 45, p.375.

[54] Bridge, *supra* n. 38, p.493.

[55] Peter Niven, Administrative Secretary, SPTL, e-mail to author, 30 May 2000.

ignore it in its entirety. In the second half of the twentieth century, the academic-legal profession in England has not only grown significantly but has become much more organized, prolific, competitive, self-assured and able to provide practitioners, and to some extent judges also, with appropriate expertise and critical advice. It would be easy to treat the convention against citation as illustrative of nothing other than judicial philistinism; yet the history of English academic law, particularly during the first half of the twentieth century, forces us to confront the question why judges might ever have cared or been expected to take advice from a profession which was so under-developed and lacking in self-confidence.

This is not, of course, to exonerate the judiciary. Other reasons for the convention against citation can be laid more or less squarely at its feet. The seventh reason for the convention is, in essence, that academic commentators are exempt from *stare decisis*. If commentary is recognized too hastily as work of authority, there is a risk that the author will change his or her mind and so render the source of law uncertain. One commentator explains the judicial predicament thus:

> "[A] work cannot be a better authority than its writer. Suppose the latter has changed his mind upon some points. What, then, are we to take as authority—the opinion expressed in a work or the later one of its author? What is the position of the judge upon whom a living authority is pressed? He, a judge, must base his opinion as a rule upon an authority, but a living person often not in a judicial situation need not".[56]

This particular argument seems to require that one makes a fuss about next to nothing. Where an author changes his or her mind on a point of law, this may simply indicate that the judge who accepted the author's original position had, like the author, made a mistake. An author's change of mind will sometimes follow a change of law, and so will suggest not that the judge has made a mistake but that the law has moved on since the time of the decision. On occasion, it might even be the case that it is the change of mind that represents the mistake and that the judge, having accepted the author's original argument, continues to subscribe to the more compelling point of view. Whatever the scenario, the argument that the integrity of the judicial process might somehow be put at risk when judges rely on viewpoints which may change seems rather feeble.

[56] Borris M. Komar, "Text-Books as Authority in Anglo-American Law" (1923) 11 *Calif. L. Rev.* 397 at 403; and cf. *Ford Motor Co. Ltd.* v. *A.E.F.* [1969] 2 All ER 481, 491, QBD (per Geoffrey Lane J).

The eighth reason for the convention is perhaps the most interesting reason. It might be summarized thus: judges ought to be wary of relying on the works of living commentators—indeed, it is unrealistic to believe that such commentators can be of all that much assistance to judges—because the two groups inhabit distinct legal worlds and are engaged in very different enterprises. If taken to its logical conclusion (though none of its proponents does appear to take it to its logical conclusion) this argument cautions against the admission of any academic commentary into court, whether the commentator be alive or dead. H. G. Hanbury wrote in 1958 of how "[t]he attitude of the Bench" towards university lawyers was "far more favourable than was the case twenty or even ten years ago". Judges, he added, were beginning to "regard teachers and writers as friends and colleagues".[57] In his address to the SPTL during the same year, however, Devlin J set out to charm his audience with a confession that makes one shudder at the thought of what judicial attitudes towards academics must have been like a decade or so earlier:

> "[I]t has always struck me as odd that students of law and academic lawyers tend to avoid the criminal law, comparatively speaking, and interest themselves so much in the civil law. Of course it is an easier job, if I may put it that way inoffensively; you have the decisions of the Court of Appeal and the House of Lords and the function of the academic lawyer is that of the critic of finer points of play".[58]

Not only, in other words, is the commentary of jurists parasitic upon the work of judges but it is essentially an exercise in critique; and critique comes cheap: the consequences of an academic producing misconceived criticism will be nowhere near as serious as the consequences of a judge committing errors in the process of decision-making. The theme is elaborated by Megarry in his Hamlyn lectures of 1962. Rejecting the proposal that some academic lawyers might, like practising barristers, be appointed as judges, Megarry argues that whereas the barrister spends "much of his life in the law . . . among the facts . . . [t]he academic lawyer escapes all this":[59]

[57] Harold Greville Hanbury, *The Vinerian Chair and Legal Education* (Oxford, Basil Blackwell, 1958), p.244.

[58] Patrick Devlin, "Statutory Offences" (1958) n.s. 4 *J.S.P.T.L.* 206 at 206–7; repr. in his *Samples of Lawmaking* (London, Oxford University Press, 1962), pp.67–82 at 69.

[59] R. E. Megarry, *Lawyer and Litigant in England* (London, Stevens & Sons, 1962), p.120.

"When an experienced advocate becomes a judge, he has experienced so much advocacy that he has it in his bones to make suitable discounts, to detect and check any undesirable practices, and to come as close to the truth as is likely to be possible for any human tribunal. The admission in cross-examination that was obtained in reply to a loaded question, the answer that was begotten of confusion rather than confession, the moment of truth, all these he has learned to recognise and evaluate: of all of these, and a mass of practical and procedural detail, the academic lawyer is innocent".[60]

To be a trial judge demands a certain nous which comes from experience in the trenches. Academic lawyers never obtain the experience and so necessarily lack the nous. What, then, of the possibility that academics might sit as appellate judges? Again, Megarry is convinced that the requisite qualities would be absent:

"The didactic life of a lecturer and author is far removed from the strife of debate and contention. The tempo of life is quite different. It is one thing for ideas and theories to evolve and be tested over the years in the study and the lecture-room, and another thing to judge competing theories in the hot-house of the court-room . . . I would also harbour the suspicion that the academic mind, accustomed to contemplating the great verities of the law, might recoil from the great bulk of the humdrum work, devoid of academic interest and ranging over territory little honoured in the academic world, which forms the daily fare of even appellate courts".[61]

The argument that judges must regularly deliberate in the face of institutional and temporal constraints rarely encountered in academic life is one which is often made by jurists with experience in practice or on the bench.[62] Megarry makes this argument but also goes further: the academic lawyer, he is claiming, is likely to be too ponderous, leisurely, genteel, impractical and unworldly to be able to carry out the work of a judge. Faced with such work, the legal academic would probably prove unreliable or crack under pressure. The claim, again, is that academics have the easier job.

That someone could make this claim and then be elected three years later as President of the SPTL perhaps provides some insight into the collective psyche of the English academic-legal profession during this

[60] *Ibid.*, pp.120–1.

[61] *Ibid.*, pp.121–2. See also Laski to Holmes, 13 May 1933, in *Holmes-Laski Letters*, *supra* n. 48, II, p.1439.

[62] See, e.g., Sir Leslie Scarman, "Law Reform—Lessons From English Experience" (1968) 3 *Manitoba L. J.* 47 at 57–8; and also, in the American context, Thurman Arnold, "Professor Hart's Theology" (1960) 73 *Harv. L. Rev.* 1298.

period.[63] In *Cordell* v. *Second Clanfield Properties* (1969), Megarry, by this point elevated to the bench, adapts his general line of argument in order to explain why judges ought to be circumspect when relying on the opinions of commentators:

> "The process of authorship is entirely different from that of judicial decision. The author, no doubt, has the benefit of a broad and comprehensive survey of his chosen subject as a whole, together with a lengthy period of gestation, and intermittent opportunities for reconsideration. But he is exposed to the peril of yielding to preconceptions, and he lacks the advantage of that impact and sharpening of focus which the detailed facts of a particular case bring to the judge. Above all, he has to form his ideas without the purifying ordeal of skilled argument on the specific facts of a contested case. Argued law is tough law. This is as true today as it was in 1409 when Hankford J. said: "Home ne scaveroit de quel metal une campane fuit, si ceo ne fuit batu, quasi diceret, le ley per bon disputacion serra bien conus" [Just as a man would not know the quality of a bell without ringing it thoroughly, so too it is said that by good disputing shall the law be well known] (Y.B. 11 Hen. 4, Mich., fo. 37); and these words are none the less apt for a judge who sits, as I do, within earshot of the bells of St. Clements. I would, therefore, give credit to the words of any reputable author in book or article as expressing tenable and arguable ideas, as fertilisers of thought, and as conveniently expressing the fruits of research in print, often in apt and persuasive language. But I would do no more than that; and in particular I would expose those views to the testing and refining process of argument".[64]

Juristic reasoning is different from, and invariably inferior to, judicial reasoning because it is insufficiently honed through disputation. Citation of academic commentary in court ought to arouse judicial suspicion—so the argument goes—because such commentary tends to come wrapped in cotton wool, rarely if ever having been subjected to robust scrutiny. Just as academic lawyers themselves are likely to be temperamentally unsuited to judicial tasks, many of their arguments and theories will be too fragile for the real world of the courtroom.

Megarry was probably quite right to claim that neither academics nor their arguments would often have made a favourable impression in court—he was writing, after all, during that period when the academic legal profession was still nascent and somewhat complacent. The

[63] Megarry served as President of the SPTL for 1965–66. On the type of academic mentality in question here, see Stanley Fish, *There's No Such Thing as Free Speech and it's a Good Thing, Too* (New York, Oxford University Press, 1994), pp.273–9.

[64] *Cordell* v. *Second Clanfield Properties Ltd* [1969] 2 Ch. 9, 16–17.

objective here is not to dispute his claim, or, for that matter, the arguments of anyone else who expresses misgivings about academics and legal commentary finding their way into the courtroom. What concerns us is the signal which this general line of reasoning sends out. If one reflects upon the convention against citation, and upon the reasons adduced to explain that convention, what impression of academic lawyers is one likely to form? The answer seems to be: that they are, variously, delicate plants, loose cannons, an uncharismatic and whimsical bunch, unable to be trusted not to change their minds on points of law and unlikely to be able to perform the role of a judge; that they are sometimes too ponderous, at other times too expeditious, in articulating legal opinions; that they have the easy life of the armchair critic, under no pressure to provide solutions quickly and accountable to no-one should their solutions prove wrongheaded; that their work ideally ought not to be treated as secondary authority, or, if it is to be treated thus, must be used with circumspection; and that their influence on counsel, should they ever have any, ought to be deemed undeserving of acknowledgement. Small wonder that English academic lawyers in the past have, with regard to the courts, seemed somewhat attention-starved and blighted by a sense of inferiority.

SILVER LININGS

This chapter has opened with a bleak picture of an earlier era. The good news is that this picture provides only a small element of the story. There is evidence that, as compared with the courts of this earlier period, the English appeal courts of the late twentieth century became generally more receptive to, and more willing to acknowledge the influence of, academic opinion. This part of the story will be considered in the next section. The present section focuses on the part of the story which has attracted the least attention, which to a large extent has been overlooked, and yet which is the most intriguing. This part of the story might be summarized thus: the English courts were never resolutely committed to the convention against citation, and the support that did exist for the convention could not prevent certain jurists from influencing judicial decision-making. Each of these claims requires elaboration. In providing support for the second claim I shall take the same approach as was adopted in Chapter 4 and focus primarily on the phenomenon of case note writing.

Better read when dead?

Evidence of English courts relying explicitly on the commentaries of living authors can be traced at least as far back as the early nineteenth century. In *Taylor* v. *Curtis* (1816), it was noted that "[b]ooks of living authors are not usually to be cited", suggesting that the convention might admit of exceptions.[65] One such exception was made four years later in *Cholmondeley* v. *Clinton*, in which Plumer, MR, treated as authority commentary by the then Lord Chancellor of Ireland, Lord Redesdale.[66] Instances of nineteenth century courts citing living commentators are fairly abundant.[67] During the twentieth century, such instances became ever more abundant. Throughout the last two decades of his life, Pollock, about whom we will have more to say in a moment, would appear quite regularly in judicial opinions.[68] "His writings", according to one commentator, "were cited in court probably more than any other writings in their authors' lifetime".[69] Dicey was likewise quite often cited in court during his lifetime (although he was not accorded the same stature as was Pollock),[70] as were certain jurists of the following generation.[71] It also became more common, as

[65] *Taylor* v. *Curtis* (1816) 6 Taunt. 608, 610; 128 Eng. Rep. 1172, 1173; and cf. also *Johnes* v. *Johnes* (1814) 3 Dow 1, 15; 3 Eng. Rep. 969, 974 ("one who had held no judicial situation could not regularly be mentioned as an authority").

[66] *Cholmondeley* v. *Clinton* (1820) 2 Jac. & W. 1, 151–2; 37 Eng. Rep. 527, 581–2.

[67] Eleven such instances are listed in Komar, *supra* n. 56, pp.403–4.

[68] See, e.g., *Admiralty Commissioners* v. *S.S. Amerika* [1917] AC 38, 59, HL (per Lord Sumner); *Performing Right Society Ltd.* v. *Mitchell and Booker (Palais de Danse) Ltd.* [1924] 1 KB 762, 767–8 (per McCardle J.); *Haynes* v. *Harwood* [1935] 1 KB 146, 163–4 (per Maugham LJ).

[69] O. Hood Phillips, "Legal Authors Since 1800", in *Then and Now, 1799–1974: Commemorating 175 Years of Law Bookselling and Publishing* (London, Sweet & Maxwell, 1974), pp.3–30 at 23.

[70] See, e.g., *Rex* v. *Albany* [1915] 3 KB 716, 726 (per Darling J); *In re De Keyser's Royal Hotel Ltd.* [1919] 2 Ch. 197, 205, CA (*arguendo*). In the House of Lords' judgment in the latter case, Lord Dunedin refers to Dicey, but avoids mentioning his name: *A.-G.* v. *De Keyser's Royal Hotel* [1920] AC 508, 526 ("The prerogative is defined by a learned constitutional writer"). Sir Neville Faulks recounts that when he and Cyril (later Lord) Salmon served together as counsel before the House of Lords in the case of *Hill* v. *William Hill (Park Lane) Ltd* [1949] AC 530, their attempt to cite Dicey (d. 1922) was resisted by Viscount Jowitt LC " 'What', said Lord Jowitt on the woolsack, 'have the views of Professor Dicey to do with us? Is he an authority?' . . . I [had] obviously made an ass of myself": Neville Faulks, *No Mitigating Circumstances* (London, William Kimber, 1977), pp.113–14. Perhaps not surprisingly, the intervention does not appear in the case report.

[71] See, e.g., *Read* v. *J. Lyons & Co. Ltd.* [1945] KB 216, 236, per Scott LJ (CA); *Howard* v. *Walker* [1947] KB 860, 863 (per Lord Goddard CJ); and also Carey Miller, *supra* n. 4, p.240; Birks, *supra* n. 4, p.165.

the twentieth century progressed, for counsel to be able to refer explicitly to the work of living commentators without any judicial objection being raised.[72] In 1947, in a by no means uncritical review of *Winfield on Tort*, Denning J declared that:

> "The reason why such books are so useful in the Courts is that they are not digests of cases but repositories of principles. They are written by men who have studied the law as a science with more detachment than is possible to men engaged in busy practice. The influence of the academic lawyers is greater now than it has ever been and is greater than they themselves realise. Their influence is largely through their writings. The notion that their works are not of authority except after the author's death has long been exploded".[73]

Our earlier discussion of the stubborn persistence of the convention against citation suggests that the last sentence in this quotation was probably over-optimistic. Denning himself, none the less, was characteristically unafraid to rub against the grain. Commenting, in 1957, on the Court of Appeal decision in *Ashdown* v. *Samuel Williams & Sons*,[74] L. C. B. Gower had lamented that:

> "the case affords a typical illustration of the English practitioners' lack of interest in periodical literature. Some time before the appeal was argued the decision in the court of first instance had been the subject of lengthy notes, by Professor Goodhart in the *Law Quarterly Review*, and in this *Review*. Neither note was cited and plaintiff's counsel was not even aware of them. This would not occur, I believe, anywhere else in the civilised world. In some of the Dominions, for example, the notes would have been referred to and replied to in the judgments themselves. I am not complaining; we do things

[72] See, e.g., *Re O'Keefe* [1940] 1 Ch. 124 (Crossman J accepting counsel's citations of both Cheshire and Dicey on conflict of laws as correct statements of the law); *R.* v. *Newland* [1954] 1 QB 158, 162 (CCA); *Re Ellenborough Park* [1956] 1 Ch. 131, 163 (CA); *Rookes* v. *Barnard* [1964] AC 1129, 1141 (HL); and also Paterson, *supra* n. 20, p.16.

[73] A. T. Denning, Book Review (1947) 63 *L.Q.R.* 516. It is worth speculating at this juncture that the convention against citing living authors may have been subverted owing to the fact that, at certain points in the past, various works authored by eminent jurists long dead (and therefore citable) have fallen into the hands of modern editors. Although such works will more often than not be associated solely with the names of their originators, where canonical texts have been substantially modernized by later authors we sometimes find, even before judicial support for the convention against citation began to diminish, courts allowing (perhaps we would do better to say not forbidding) explicit reference to living jurists.

[74] *Ashdown* v. *Samuel Williams & Sons* [1957] 1 QB 409.

differently here. But if practitioners choose to ignore academic writings they must not complain if academics criticise the result".[75]

In *White* v. *Blackmore*, Denning, who had presided over Gower's inaugural lecture in 1950, noted the latter's criticisms of *Ashdown* v. *Williams* and remarked not only that he was "disposed to agree with them" but that he considered it unfortunate that they "were not brought to our attention".[76] While the more common judicial approach was to admonish counsel for bringing the commentary of living academics into the courtroom, Denning in this instance did quite the opposite. That he should have adopted such an approach is not surprising; as a barrister, he had successfully cited the work of a living jurist before the Court of Appeal—indeed, he claimed that his citation of the work in question significantly influenced the decision in the immediate case and in future cases.[77] The law reviews, he asserted in 1984, "are baskets full of the fruits of research. Some of the fruit is good and fit to pick".[78] The very best "articles and contributions to these reviews", he had claimed over thirty years earlier, "have a considerable influence". Not only do they sometimes contain "[p]oints which escape the advocate in the case", but "[c]urrent decisions are discussed and their correctness canvassed. The result is that when the cases reach the appellate Courts, the judges have the benefit of these criticisms before them".[79] Asked why he thought the House of Lords had, in *Hedley Byrne* v. *Heller*,[80] accepted and extended his dissenting judgment in *Candler* v. *Crane, Christmas & Co.*[81] on the issue of liability for negligent misstatements, Denning's answer was blunt: "The commentators helped a lot. They had made useful criticisms. Those things do

[75] L. C. B. G., "Tortfeasors' Charter Upheld" (1957) 20 *M.L.R.* 181 at 183. The note in the *Modern Law Review* on the first instance decision was also written by Gower: see L. C. B. G., "A Tortfeasors' Charter?" (1956) 19 *M.L.R.* 532.

[76] *White* v. *Blackmore* [1972] 3 All ER 158, 167 (CA).

[77] See Lord Denning, *The Discipline of Law* (London, Butterworths, 1979), pp.237–8; "The Universities and Law Reform" (1951) n.s. 1 *J.S.P.T.L.* 258 at 264–5; "1885–1984" (1984) 100 *L.Q.R.* 513 at 514 ("[W]hen I was a young K.C., I quoted the article [Arthur Goodhart] wrote in 1938 (Hospitals and Trained Nurses 54 L.Q.R. 553) to the Court of Appeal. It had a great effect on them. Their judgment is reported in *Gold* v. *Essex County Council* [1942] 2 K.B. 293. It altered the whole course of decisions on medical malpractice. All due to Arthur's article").

[78] Denning, "1885–1984", *supra* n. 77, p.513.

[79] Denning, "The Universities and Law Reform", *supra* n. 77, p.264.

[80] *Hedley Byrne & Co. Ltd.* v. *Heller & Partners Ltd.* [1964] AC 465.

[81] *Candler* v. *Crane, Christmas & Co.* [1951] KB 154 (CA).

influence even the House of Lords. The trend of other decisions likewise".[82]

We will see in due course that Pollock, more than any other jurist, appears to have been responsible for pushing the appellate courts towards the position on negligent misrepresentation adopted in *Hedley Byrne*. Before turning our attention to Pollock, however, two further observations about the convention against citation ought to be elaborated. The first of these observations is the more positive one: by the 1970s, the convention, while not quite having disappeared, was very obviously in retreat.[83] In his address to the SPTL in 1972, Lord Reid, far from speaking *de haut en bas* as Devlin J had done before the same audience in 1958, began by seeking an *entente cordiale*:

> "I am very glad to have this opportunity of meeting and exchanging views with those of you who belong to a sister branch of our profession. It is, I suppose, inevitable that opportunities for interchange should be few. The next best thing is to meet as often as we can. It is not enough that we should see each other's written work. Even that is not always easy for us. But I think we are making some progress there. In the House of Lords at least we turn a blind eye to the old rule that an academic writer is not an authority until he is dead, because then he can no longer change his mind".[84]

The argument that jurists and judges ought to try to operate in partnership would, we will see, receive yet more vigorous support—from both groups—in years to come. For the moment, the important point to note is that which is expressed in the final sentence of the quotation. The point was echoed by Lord Diplock in 1975: "judges no longer think that the sources of judicial wisdom are confined to judgments in decided cases . . . In appellate courts, at any rate, when confronted with a doubtful point of law we want to know what living academic jurists have said about it, and we consider that counsel have not done their homework unless they come equipped to tell us about this".[85] As if to illustrate this point, during the following year the House of Lords referred the case of *Oppenheimer* v. *Cattermole* back to the special commissioners for further findings as to relevant German law (the case

[82] Quoted in Roland Goldich, "Law and Social Change: An Interview with Lord Denning" (1969) 22 *King's Counsel* 6 at 8. See also Denning, *The Discipline of Law*, *supra* n. 77, p.241; and cf. Dennis R. Klinck, "'This Other Eden': Lord Denning's Pastoral Vision" (1994) 14 *Oxf. Jnl. Leg. Studs*. 25.

[83] See also Carey Miller, *supra* n. 4, p.240; Paterson, *supra* n. 20, p.17.

[84] Lord Reid, "The Judge as Law Maker" (1972) n.s. 12 *J.S.P.T.L.* 22.

[85] Diplock, *supra* n. 19, p.459.

concerned a claim of exemption from income tax by a German emigré who had become a naturalized British subject) and returned the appeal for further argument when their Lordships became aware of a recently published article by F. A. Mann which, according to Lord Cross, made it clear that "the [original] findings of the commissioners as to the relevant German law were almost certainly based on inadequate material".[86] By the closing decades of the twentieth century, English appellate judges appeared to be more receptive to academic opinion than had ever been the case before.

We will elaborate on this last proposition in the next section. But let us not jump the gun. That judges have become more willing to see living commentators cited in court—and this is our second, rather more downbeat observation—does not necessarily mean that such commentators have become more influential. To reorient a distinction often associated with Searle, judicial references to commentary are frequently not so much instances of "use" as of "mention".[87] In *Haynes* v. *Harwood*, a case concerning the defence of *volenti non fit injuria*, Greer LJ quoted a passage taken from an article by Goodhart dealing with relevant American case law and concluded that the "passage not only represents the law of the United States, but I think it also accurately represents the law of this country".[88] In the same case, Greer's reference to Goodhart is noted approvingly by Maugham LJ.[89] There is no evidence, however, that Goodhart's article in this instance influenced judicial thought. The article is cited, rather, in order to reinforce a view that both judges appear already to have held. Consider, similarly, the following reference to Goodhart by Sellers LJ in *Ingram* v. *Little*:

> "Dr. Goodhart might well be right when he said [in his article, 'Mistake as to Identity in the Law of Contract' (1941) 57 *L.Q.R.* 228] that 'There is no branch of the law of contract which is more uncertain and difficult' than that involved in the present case, and I am conscious that our decision here will not have served to dispel the uncertainty".[90]

[86] *Oppenheimer* v. *Cattermole* [1976] AC 249, 268. The relevant article, to which the House of Lords explicitly declared its indebtedness, is F. A. Mann, "The Present Validity of Nazi Nationality Laws" (1973) 89 *L.Q.R.* 194.

[87] John R. Searle, *Speech Acts: An Essay in the Philosophy of Language* (Cambridge, Cambridge University Press, 1969), pp.73–6. Searle is by no means the only philosopher to to have discussed this distinction; before Searle, it was developed by (*inter alios*) Bertrand Russell, Gilbert Ryle and P. F. Strawson.

[88] *Haynes* v. *Harwood* [1935] 1 KB 146, 157 (CA).

[89] *Ibid.*, p.162.

[90] *Ingram* v. *Little* [1960] 3 WLR 504, 513 (CA).

Again, the reference to Goodhart can hardly be said to demonstrate juristic influence. Not that this should be taken to imply that Goodhart generally failed to influence judicial decision-making. Even in *Ingram* v. *Little* there are passages which bear the mark of his thought,[91] and we shall see below that few other jurists influenced the English appeal courts to a comparable degree. We ought none the less to emphasize that, in so far as judges do cite academic commentary, they quite often cite it as a prop, or even as a foil.

Indeed English judges, like their American counterparts (see Chapter 3), sometimes refer to academic commentary not so as to acknowledge influence but to record how disappointing or misconceived they consider that commentary to be. Citing *Sudgen on Powers*, Park J declared in *Smith* v. *Doe* (1821) that although it was "a book of great authority" he was "staggered" by the argument which he found therein: were the argument to prevail, "it would invalidate nine-tenths of all the leases in the kingdom granted under powers. I can only say, such a consequence is to be deeply deplored".[92] During the twentieth century, disapproval by judges of the works of commentators tended to be just as uncompromising. In *Shenton* v. *Tyler* (1939), both Sir Wilfrid Greene MR, and Luxmoore LJ argued at length that English textbook writers were wrong in claiming that the common law treats as privileged communications between husband and wife during marriage.[93] Similarly, in the House of Lords' decision in *Button* v. *DPP* (1966) Lord Gardiner, reinforcing the argument of Marshall J in the Court of Criminal Appeal, declared that almost every English commentator from Blackstone onwards had made the mistake of assuming that an essential ingredient of affray was that the offence must occur in public.[94] Fairly regularly we find judges declaring that the textbook or commentary upon which counsel has relied is in error on the relevant point of law.[95] "This court

[91] See *ibid.*, pp.512–13.

[92] *Smith* v. *Doe* (1821) 2 Brod. & B. 473, 535; 129 Eng. Rep. 1048, 1072.

[93] *Shenton* v. *Tyler* [1939] 1 Ch. 620.

[94] *Button* v. *Director of Public Prosecutions* [1966] AC 591, 624–5. For the review by Marshall of the relevant commentaries, see *ibid.* at 607–9. The argument that commentators had mistakenly classified affray as a public offence was also advanced by counsel for the Crown: see *ibid.*, at 619–21.

[95] See, e.g., *Nissan* v. *Attorney-General* [1970] AC 179, 191 (*arguendo*), 212 (per Lord Reid) (HL); *Re Union Accident Insurance Co. Ltd* [1972] 1 All ER 1105, 1109, Ch. D. (per Plowman J); *Barclays Bank Ltd* v. *Taylor* [1972] 2 All ER 752, 757–8, Ch. D. (per Goulding J); *White* v. *Jones* [1995] 1 All ER 691, 716, HL (per Lord Browne-Wilkinson). See also *R.* v. *Secretary of State for Transport, ex parte Richmond upon Thames L.B.C.* [1994] 1 All ER 577, 597 (QBD), where Laws J argued not that the academic literature

would never hesitate to disagree with a statement in a textbook", declared Lord Goddard CJ in *Bastin* v. *Davies*, "however authoritative, or however long it had stood, if it thought right to do so".[96] When, in *Johnson* v. *Agnew*, Lord Wilberforce quoted from the fourth edition of T. Cyprian Williams's *Vendor and Purchaser*, he did so only in order to proffer his opinion that the passage reproduced was "a jumble of unclear propositions not logically related to each other" and " 'supported' by footnote references to cases . . . which are not explained or analysed".[97] It would be silly to assume that when judges cite the works of commentators, they must be treating those works as authoritative.

This last line of argument transports us back to Chapter 2, where we considered the dangers of equating citation with influence. Throughout the twentieth century, English judges became ever more willing to cite, and to see counsel cite, the works of living commentators in court. That such commentators were being cited more regularly probably indicates that, in general, they were becoming more influential. Case law reveals, nevertheless, that judges quite often cite commentary not because they are influenced by it, but because it supports a view which they already hold or even because they consider it to be wrong. Without doubt, one may be cited without being influential.

More intriguing is the proposition that commentators may be influential without being cited. Intuitively, this proposition seems entirely reasonable. But can it be substantiated? It was noted in Chapter 2 that identification of influence sometimes requires that we focus on personal qualities such as energy, diplomacy, reputation within the professional community and the like. For the remainder of this section I shall discuss two jurists whose influence on English judicial decision-making extended well beyond citations to their works.

Pollock, Goodhart and case notes

A member of a famous legal family and part of the broader Victorian intellectual aristocracy,[98] Sir Frederick Pollock was an English approx-

cited by counsel was wrong on the relevant point of law but that it could not be appropriately applied to the problem at hand; and *Henderson* v. *Merrett Syndicates Ltd* [1995] 2 AC 145, 192–3 (HL), where Lord Goff disagreed with academic criticism of Oliver J's reasoning in *Midland Bank Trust Co. Ltd.* v. *Hett, Stubbs & Kemp* [1979] Ch. 384.

[96] *Bastin* v. *Davies* [1950] 2 K.B. 579, 582–3.

[97] *Johnson* v. *Agnew*, *supra* n. 24, at 395–6.

[98] Pollock's grandfather, Sir Jonathan Frederick Pollock, was Lord Chief Baron of the

imation of what certain contemporary Americans have termed the lawyer-statesman.[99] We have noted already that, during Pollock's later years, the English courts began to accord his work a degree of authority that was normally reserved for the dead. Yet it was during an earlier period, in the aftermath of *Derry* v. *Peek*,[100] that his influence over English judges was most decisive.[101]

In *Derry* v. *Peek*, the directors of a tramway company stated in their prospectus that they had the right to use steam power; in fact, they had no such right but believed that the Board of Trade would award it to them as a matter of course. Relying on the prospectus, the respondent purchased shares in the company. Subsequently, the Board of Trade refused to award a right to use steam power to the company and it was wound up. The Court of Appeal held that the fact that there exist no reasonable grounds for believing a statement to be accurate is sufficient to establish liability for fraud. The House of Lords reversed this decision, holding that negligent misstatements were not of themselves sufficient to give rise to liability for fraud.

Pollock had welcomed the decision of the Court of Appeal.[102] Regularly, in his case notes in the *Law Quarterly Review*, he remarked that "[t]he morality of the law is . . . decidedly above the morality of ordinary mercantile life".[103] In *Derry* v. *Peek*, a case in which the

Exchequer; his father, Sir William Frederick Pollock, was Queen's Remembrancer; and his cousin, Sir Ernest Murray Pollock, became (as Lord Hanworth) Master of the Rolls. On the Victorian intellectual aristocracy, see N. G. Annan, "The Intellectual Aristocracy", in J. H. Plumb (ed.), *Studies in Social History: A Tribute to G. M. Trevelyan* (London, Longmans, Green & Co., 1955), pp.241–87; and on Pollock as part of this aristocracy, see Sir John Pollock, *Time's Chariot* (London, John Murray, 1950), p.50; H. D. Hazeltine (1937) 53 *L.Q.R.* 190–3.

[99] On this idealized figure, see William H. Rehnquist, "The Lawyer-Statesman in American History" (1986) 9 *Harvard J. Law & Pub. Pol.* 537; and, on the apparent destruction of the ideal, cf. Anthony T. Kronman, *The Lost Lawyer: Failing Ideals of the Legal Profession* (Cambridge, Mass., Belknap Press, 1993). Pollock's obituary in *The Times* records various instances in which he was called upon to provide legal advice regarding affairs of the state: see Anon., "Sir Frederick Pollock, K. C.: The 'Old Broad Culture'", *The Times*, 19 January 1937, p.14.

[100] *Derry* v. *Peek* (1889) 14 App. Cas. 337 (HL).

[101] The following discussion summarizes that to be found in Neil Duxbury, "When We Were Young: Notes in the *Law Quarterly Review*, 1885–1925" (2000) 116 *L.Q.R.* 474 at 491–3, which in turn builds upon the discussion of *Derry* v. *Peek* offered by David Sugarman, "Legal Theory, the Common Law Mind and the Making of the Textbook Tradition", in W. Twining (ed.), *Legal Theory and Common Law* (Oxford, Blackwell, 1986), pp.26–61 at 46–8.

[102] See (1888) 4 *L.Q.R.* 369; (1889) 5 *L.Q.R.* 101.

[103] (1891) 7 *L.Q.R.* 99. In much the same vein, see also (1889) 5 *L.Q.R.* 107; (1890) 6 *L.Q.R.* 462; (1892) 8 *L.Q.R.* 187; (1894) 10 *L.Q.R.* 205; (1898) 14 *L.Q.R.* 115; (1905) 21 *L.Q.R.* 102.

respondent relied upon "statements the truth of which" the company directors had "not ascertained",[104] the commercial world was receiving a small part of its come-uppance for relying on lax moral standards. When the decision of the Court of Appeal was reversed, Pollock did not mince his words: "the decision of the House of Lords has dangerously relaxed the legal conception of honesty."[105] In the years following that decision, he used the case notes section of the *Law Quarterly Review* to mount a sustained and uncompromising crusade against it.[106] "*Derry* v. *Peek*", he lamented, "is now law, though bad law",[107] for it "encourage[s] practices which may easily go to the very verge of fraud";[108] indeed, to welcome the decision would be "to confound the conclusions of common sense".[109]

Just how effective was this crusade? It is, as Sugarman notes, difficult to tell.[110] What is clear is that the case notes were only part of the initiative. Pollock predictably excoriated the House of Lords' decision in his 1890 edition of *The Law of Torts*.[111] In that same year, Parliament expressed its dissatisfaction over the decision.[112] The Law Lords who decided *Derry* v. *Peek* were all common lawyers, furthermore, and their decision was ill-received among Chancery judges.[113] In 1893, Pollock rejoiced in a letter to Holmes that "[m]y enemy *Derry* v. *Peek* has not been so much as cited in court here—certainly nothing like a judicial discussion".[114] In time, of course, the House of Lords itself would limit the scope of *Derry* v. *Peek*—most famously in 1963,[115] but

[104] (1889) 5 *L.Q.R.* 102.

[105] Frederick Pollock, "*Derry* v. *Peek* in the House of Lords" (1889) 5 *L.Q.R.* 410 at 422.

[106] See, e.g., (1890) 6 *L.Q.R.* 112; (1891) 7 *L.Q.R.* 5, 107, 309–10; (1896) 12 *L.Q.R.* 205; (1899) 15 *L.Q.R.* 236; (1900) 16 *L.Q.R.* 217; (1907) 23 *L.Q.R.* 133; (1911) 27 *L.Q.R.* 276.

[107] (1892) 8 *L.Q.R.* 7.

[108] (1893) 9 *L.Q.R.* 202.

[109] (1892) 8 *L.Q.R.* 113.

[110] Sugarman, *supra* n. 101, p.47.

[111] See Sir Frederick Pollock, *The Law of Torts: A Treatise on the Principles of Obligations Arising from Civil Wrongs in the Common Law* (2nd. edn., London, Stevens & Sons, 1890), pp.254 *et seq.*

[112] See the Directors' Liability Act 1890, s. 3(1) (imposing a statutory duty of care on those who issue prospectuses).

[113] See W. R. Cornish and G. de N. Clark, *Law and Society in England, 1750–1950* (London, Sweet & Maxwell, 1989), p.221.

[114] Pollock to Holmes, 11 December 1893, in M. DeWolfe Howe (ed.), *The Pollock-Holmes Letters: Correspondence of Sir Frederick Pollock and Mr. Justice Holmes, 1874–1932*, 2 vols. (Cambridge, Cambridge University Press, 1942), I, p.49.

[115] See *Hedley Byrne* v. *Heller*, *supra* n. 80, in particular at 610 (per Lord Devlin), and cf. (1907) 23 *L.Q.R.* 133. Recall also the quotation from Lord Denning accompanying n. 82, *supra*.

more significantly for our purposes in the case of *Nocton* v. *Ashburton* (1914) when, led by the then Lord Chancellor, Viscount Haldane, their Lordships (by this stage a far more Chancery-minded group) decided *inter alia* that, *Derry* v. *Peek* notwithstanding, relief for loss incurred owing to innocent misrepresentations by fiduciaries may still be available in equity.[116] Although, not surprisingly, no reference is made in *Nocton* v. *Ashburton* to Pollock's campaign against *Derry* v. *Peek*, it is noted that the latter case "is in some quarters thought to have introduced a far-reaching change into the law",[117] that "[i]t has been the subject of much comment"[118] and accepted "in certain quarters under protest".[119] Pollock expressed delight at the decision.[120] This was hardly surprising, for he had been active behind the scenes:

> "Haldane asked me last week to a tobacco talk of *Derry* v. *Peek* and the possibility of minimizing its consequences. The Lords are going to hold that it does not apply to the situation created by a positive fiduciary duty such as a solicitor's, in other words, go as near as they dare to saying it was wrong, as all in Lincoln's Inn thought at the time".[121]

If anything might be deduced from this chapter as it has progressed so far, it ought to be that the conventions of judges with regard to what might count as presentable authority have traditionally operated largely to conceal the influence of academic writers on English case law. As regards the gradual movement away from the House of Lords' decision in *Derry* v. *Peek*, we simply do not know just how involved or influential Pollock would have been. But it is clear that his opinion was valued and sought out, and that the reach of the decision was ultimately restricted in a manner congenial to his wishes. The lesson here is obvious. We saw in Chapter 2 that motives for citing are complex, and that the extent to which a source has proved influential cannot necessarily be deduced from the degree to which it has been cited. Non-citation of sources, conversely, ought not to compel the conclusion that those sources must be without influence.

Arthur Lehman Goodhart was born in 1891, two years after the House of Lords' decision in *Derry* v. *Peek*. If Pollock was an English

[116] See *Nocton* v. *Lord Ashburton* [1914] AC 932 at 946–56; and cf. also *Candler* v. *Crane, Christmas & Co.*, *supra* n. 81, at 177–8 (per Denning LJ, dissenting).

[117] *Nocton* v. *Ashburton*, *ibid.*, p.969 (per Lord Shaw).

[118] *Ibid.*, p.946 (per Viscount Haldane).

[119] *Ibid.*, p.970 (per Lord Shaw).

[120] Frederick Pollock, "*Nocton* v. *Lord Ashburton*" (1915) 31 *L.Q.R.* 93.

[121] Pollock to Holmes, 20 May 1914, in *Pollock-Holmes Letters*, *supra* n. 114, I, p.215.

approximation of the lawyer-statesman, Goodhart, as is obvious from his *vitae* in *Who Was Who*, was the genuine article. An American by birth, he spent nearly all of his professional career in England. In 1931, he gave up his fellowship at Corpus Christi College, Cambridge, in order to become Professor of Jurisprudence at Oxford, a post which he held for twenty years. Goodhart would have been more suited to, indeed would have preferred, the Vinerian Chair: essentially a common lawyer with jurisprudential interests, his credentials as a legal philosopher were quite often disparaged—Harold Laski, Roscoe Pound and Felix Frankfurter all remarked on what they considered to be his lack of intellectual flair.[122] Goodhart's unexceptional reputation as a legal philosopher was more than offset, however, by the praise and affection bestowed upon him by many of England's senior lawyers and judges. Various judicial assessments of the man and his work have been noted here already. "The essays of Professor Goodhart have had a decisive influence in many important decisions", wrote Alfred Denning in 1947.[123] Almost forty years later he proclaimed Goodhart to be "[b]eyond doubt the greatest living jurist of our time".[124] Judges would quite regularly declare their indebtedness to him.[125] If it were possible to mount an appeal from the House of Lords, one Scottish judge joked, it would be to Goodhart.[126] He was, according to Lord Reid, the jurist whose commentaries would make judges "sit up and take note".[127]

[122] For the observation that "Goodhart himself felt that he would be happier with the Vinerian Chair", see Robert F. V. Heuston, "Goodhart, Arthur Lehman", in A. W. B. Simpson (ed.), *Biographical Dictionary of the Common Law* (London, Butterworths, 1984), pp.211–212 at 212. On Goodhart as common lawyer, see Anon., "Professor A. L. Goodhart: Influence on Law in Britain" (obituary), *The Times*, 11 November 1978, p.16 ("It was his achievement to introduce the common law into jurisprudence, or rather to show that the principles of the common law were capable of yielding to jurisprudential analysis"). For disparagement by Laski, see Laski to Holmes, 13 January 1932, in *Holmes-Laski Letters*, *supra* n. 48, II, p.1357 ("I read . . . Goodhart's *Legal Essays* and those of C. K. Allen, but I thought both of them flat beer. Neither had the trick of reaching the jugular and both were intolerably long-winded. Why cannot England produce jurists of the first order?"). And for disparagement by Pound and Frankfurter, see Richard A. Cosgrove, *Our Lady the Common Law: An Anglo-American Legal Community, 1870–1930* (New York, New York University Press, 1987), pp.197–8. See also William Twining, "Academic Law and Legal Philosophy: The Significance of Herbert Hart" (1979) *95 L.Q.R. 557* at 559.

[123] Denning, *supra* n. 73, p.516.

[124] Denning, "1885–1984", *supra* n. 77, p.514.

[125] See, e.g., *Ingram* v. *Little*, *supra* n. 90, p.512 (per Sellers LJ).

[126] Lord President Cooper, as reported by T. B. Smith, "Authors and Authority" (1972) n.s. 12 *J.S.P.T.L.* 3 at 6 ("The late Lord President . . . held that, if appeal lay from the House of Lords, it was to the Editor of the Law Quarterly Review").

[127] As reported in Paterson, *supra* n. 20, p.19.

Many of the Law Lords, one High Court judge is reported to have remarked, would "pay tremendous attention to Goodhart".[128] Even judges who were inclined to look down on university lawyers tended to regard him as an exception. Patrick Devlin, having studied under Goodhart, opened his *Samples of Lawmaking* with a tribute to his former teacher as "the one who . . . speaks with great authority in the legal world".[129] Robert Megarry, who for some twenty-five years assisted Goodhart in editing the *Law Quarterly Review*, dedicated his *Miscellany-at-Law*[130] to "Arturo Lehman Goodhart: amico optimo auctori consili prudentissimo" (a very good friend and a very wise author and adviser). "As friend and confidant of so many of the judiciary", Lord Diplock observed, "he was, perhaps, the first to move so easily between University and Inn of Court and bridge the gulf between the science and the practice of the law".[131]

Note the theme of friendship. Goodhart was very much regarded as the judge's friend. He was, in this sense, very different from Pollock. Lawson has written of "Pollock's well-known difficulty of making oral communication with anyone with whom he was not naturally *en rapport*"[132] and that Goodhart not only knew Pollock professionally but "as far as was humanly possible, as a person".[133] This last remark speaks volumes about both men: Pollock was notoriously taciturn, Goodhart especially adept at befriending those who were inclined to aloofness. Just as he could win over Pollock—whose recommendation ensured that Goodhart became editor of the *Law Quarterly Review* in 1926[134]—he was able to earn the trust and respect of a judiciary which had not been particularly inclined to acknowledge debts to and admiration for living jurists. Various commentaries on Goodhart imply that he was a master-opportunist who put to good use his inherited wealth. While at Corpus Christi, he not only edited but also financed the establishment of the *Cambridge Law Journal*.[135] According to his *Times* obituarist, he endeavoured to emphasize his jurisprudential interests in

[128] As reported in Paterson, *ibid*., p.222 n. 50.

[129] Devlin, *Samples of Lawmaking*, *supra* n. 58, p.1. The book is dedicated to Goodhart.

[130] See *supra* n. 18.

[131] Diplock, *supra* n. 19, p.459.

[132] F. H. Lawson, *The Oxford Law School, 1850–1965* (Oxford, Clarendon Press, 1968), pp.72–3.

[133] F. H. Lawson, "A. L. G.: A Professor's View" (1975) 91 *L.Q.R*. 461 at 462.

[134] See Anon., "Professor A. L. Goodhart: Influence on Law in Britain", *supra* n. 122.

[135] *Ibid*. Goodhart edited the *Cambridge Law Journal*, at first solely and then in collaboration with H. E. Salt, between 1921 and 1925.

order to improve his chances of moving to Oxford (a claim which seems questionable).[136] A renowned host and clearly blessed with great charm, he cultivated the friendship of judges and was known to be close to several Law Lords.[137] Indeed, his relationships with English judges appear to have been closer than any established by other jurists. Nobody else has been to the judiciary quite the sounding-board, quite the confidant, that Goodhart was.

One may be forgiven for considering this profile of Goodhart to be rather catty. It is certainly not entirely convincing. Contriving to impress, it was argued in Chapter 2, can prove thoroughly unimpressive. Since influence is often a by-product of other qualities, it tends to elude those who try to isolate and cultivate it. The idea that Goodhart might have been able to deploy his considerable wealth and charm so as to gain the affection and even the admiration of certain judges is vaguely plausible. Distinctly less plausible, however, is the argument that Goodhart's wealth and charm would have made him influential among judges. The point is not that these attributes would have been unhelpful, but that they alone cannot explain his peculiar position of influence. Such an explanation requires that certain other factors be taken into account.

Goodhart's position as a jurist was, as Lawson has remarked, peculiarly mid-Atlantic.[138] Certain judges seemed willing to listen to him because he could offer a transatlantic perspective on legal problems. He often criticized judicial reasoning with a robustness which was, in his time, far more American than English;[139] yet this robustness did not repel judges, for Goodhart's criticisms were always lucid, constructive,

[136] Goodhart's *Times* obituary reports (*ibid.*) that although he preferred to teach common law, he moved into the field of jurisprudence because Oxford's teacher of jurisprudence had been killed in the war, thus providing an opportunity for Goodhart to move to Oxford. Goodhart moved to Oxford between the wars when Carleton Kemp Allen (d. 1966) resigned in 1931. One of his most significant jurisprudential essays appeared in 1929: see A. L. Goodhart, "Recent Tendencies in English Jurisprudence" (1929) 7 *Canadian Bar Rev.* 275; repr. in his *Essays in Jurisprudence and the Common Law* (Cambridge, Cambridge University Press, 1931), pp.27–49.

[137] Goodhart's hospitality is remarked upon by Diplock, *supra* n. 19, p.459; and by Lawson, *supra* n. 133, p.463. Even Laski, whose low opinion of Goodhart's legal scholarship has already been noted (*supra* n. 122), could not help finding him likeable in person: Laski to Holmes, 13 July 1925, in *Holmes-Laski Letters*, *supra* n. 48, I, p.764. For Goodhart as the judge's friend, see Tony Honoré, "Goodhart, Arthur Lehman", in *D.N.B. (1971–1980)*, pp.350–1 at 350; and Paterson, *supra* n. 20, p.222 n. 51 (noting friendship with Law Lords).

[138] Lawson, *supra* n. 133, p.462.

[139] Honoré, *supra* n. 137, p.350.

polite, urbane (but not sarcastic) and grounded in common sense.[140] His skills as a critic served him well as editor of and principal case note writer for the *Law Quarterly Review* (a position which he held for some forty-five years). As editor, he ensured that even the most serious criticisms of the law were written in a respectful tone, a fact which did not go unappreciated by the judiciary.[141] His accomplishments as a case note writer were still more significant. Producing, on average, a dozen notes for each issue of the journal, Goodhart's case commentaries are often considered to be his most distinctive and influential contribution to legal studies.[142] Summarizing Goodhart's achievements as a writer of case notes, his *Times* obituarist observed that:

> "No academic lawyer, with the possible exception of his predecessor [on the *Law Quarterly Review*], Sir Frederick Pollock, ever had such a profound effect upon the law of this country. In one single year, for example, two major changes occurred, which were due in no small measure to [Goodhart's] persistent recommendation: the final establishment of reasonable foreseeability as a test for remoteness of damage in negligence, and a power given to the (then) Court of Criminal Appeal to order a new trial in certain cases".[143]

The final part of this quotation needs to be approached with care: while Goodhart regularly used his case notes to lobby for the establishment of a power in the Court of Criminal Appeal to order a new trial,[144] it is conceded by possibly his most ardent eulogist that Goodhart's campaign on this particular point was not especially successful.[145] The preceding passage of the quotation, however, concerning the test of reasonable foreseeability, is rather more interesting. Just as Pollock used the case notes section of the *Law Quarterly Review* to crusade against the House of Lords' decision in *Derry* v. *Peek*,

[140] See *ibid*.; also Heuston, *supra* n. 122, p.212.

[141] See Diplock, *supra* n. 19, pp.459–60; Paterson, *supra* n. 20, p.15.

[142] See, e.g., P. V. Baker, "A. L. G.: An Editor's View" (1975) 91 *L.Q.R.* 463 at 464, 466–8; Heuston, *supra* n. 122, p.212; Honoré, *supra* n. 137, p.350 ("[I]t was his case-notes, concise and going straight to the heart of a matter that had, rightly, the greatest impact").

[143] Anon., "Professor A. L. Goodhart: Influence on Law in Britain", *supra* n. 122.

[144] See, e.g., (1944) 60 *L.Q.R.* 33, 135; (1948) 64 *L.Q.R.* 11; (1952) 68 *L.Q.R.* 327; (1960) 76 *L.Q.R.* 192.

[145] See Baker, *supra* n. 142, p.465; though it ought to be noted that eventually, with the enactment of the Criminal Appeals Act 1964, the Court of Criminal Appeal was invested with the power to order retrials: for discussion, see Richard Nobles and David Schiff, *Understanding Miscarriages of Justice: Law, the Media and the Inevitability of Crisis* (Oxford, Oxford University Press, 2000), pp.62–9.

Goodhart used the section to attack the decision of the Court of Appeal in 1921 that negligent wrongdoers should be held liable for all direct consequences of their, or their agent's, actions, even if those consequences were not reasonably foreseeable.[146] As with Pollock's campaign, Goodhart's seemed to meet with considerable success.

In *Re Polemis*, the decision in question, stevedores employed by the charterers of a ship negligently caused a plank to fall into the ship's hold, which contained tins of petrol. A fire ensued because a spark caused by the plank's impact in the hold ignited the petrol vapour. Although it could reasonably have been anticipated that the falling of the plank would cause some damage, the specific damage that occurred was not foreseeable. Notwithstanding that the damage incurred could not be anticipated, the Court of Appeal unanimously held that the charterers were liable for the loss of the ship. Although the leading judgment in *Re Polemis* relied heavily on the eleventh edition of Pollock's *The Law of Torts*,[147] Pollock himself considered the decision most unwelcome. Not only, he argued, were all of the judgments scant and lacking in critical discussion ("[t]he Lords Justices quote the opinions on which they rely, and say nothing of . . . ones which are hardly consistent with their view") but they were also unnecessarily abstruse:

> "The judgments touch more or less on the questions of terminology which beset the adjectives 'natural', 'probable', and 'proximate'. But, with great respect, the question accepted as correct when and so far as the existence of liability is wholly in dispute—namely: Is the damage such as the defendant could reasonably be expected to anticipate?—avoids all these niceties of words. It says nothing about nature or probability, and steers clear of the philosophers' controversies on the relation of cause and effect. It is a question intelligible to plain men, even if they do not always agree in their answers in the particular case.[148]

Pollock's view of the *Polemis* decision was echoed by Goodhart. Fifty years after the decision, he wrote of how academic lawyers showed enthusiasm for it because "only the best pupils could understand it", which meant that the decision "furnished useful problems for examination papers".[149] Although the complexity of the decision may have been welcomed by law teachers, "both the Bench and the Bar", he

[146] *Re Polemis* [1921] 3 KB 560.
[147] See *ibid.*, pp.569–70 (per Bankes LJ).
[148] Frederick Pollock, "Liability for Consequences" (1922) 38 *L.Q.R.* 165 at 166–7.
[149] (1970) 86 *L.Q.R.* 454.

wrote in 1928, "are hesitant in citing and applying that most unsatisfactory case".[150] Indeed the tendency, he proclaimed, is for "judges and counsel" to "ignore *Re Polemis*".[151] "[N]o two expositors are in agreement concerning its provisions, and they differ also concerning the circumstances in which it is applicable."[152] Commenting in 1954 on the decision of the Court of Appeal in *Roe* v. *Minister of Health*,[153] Goodhart applauded Denning LJ's conclusion that the approach to liability for consequences adopted in *Re Polemis* was inordinately complex and that in many cases the courts need do no more than ask whether the consequence fell within the risk and to answer the question by applying common sense. "This", Goodhart added, "is the conclusion for which we have contended during many years, because law ought to be common sense and not a series of convoluted theorems which no two judges or textbook writers interpret in the same way".[154] Rather than resorting to such theorems, the courts ought "to concentrate on the comparatively simple problem: did the defendant take reasonable care to avoid the foreseeable consequences?"[155] The test for liability ought to be quite straightforward: "[a] tortfeasor should only be held liable for those consequences . . . which a reasonable man placed in his position would have foreseen as possible and would have avoided by due care".[156]

Thus it is that Goodhart, primarily via the case notes section of the *Law Quarterly Review*, regularly questioned the wisdom of *Re Polemis*. Not everyone found his campaign convincing.[157] Yet it seemed to make an impression on, and certainly reflected the sentiments of, some senior members of the judiciary. In 1952, Goodhart pulled together his criticisms of the *Polemis* decision in a lengthy article in the *Law Quarterly Review*.[158] First of all, he reiterated Pollock's

[150] (1928) 44 *L.Q.R.* 142.

[151] *Ibid.*, p.143.

[152] A. L. Goodhart, "Liability and Compensation" (1960) 76 *L.Q.R.* 567 at 568.

[153] *Roe* v. *Minister of Health* [1954] 2 WLR 915.

[154] (1954) 70 *L.Q.R.* 306.

[155] (1970) 86 *L.Q.R.* 454.

[156] Goodhart, "Liability for the Consequences of a 'Negligent Act'" (1926), in his *Essays in Jurisprudence and the Common Law*, *supra* n. 136, pp.110–128 at 126.

[157] See, e.g., H. L. A. Hart and Tony Honoré, *Causation in the Law* (2nd edn., Oxford, Clarendon Press, 1985; 1st edn. publ. 1959), pp.254–75; and cf. Goodhart, *supra* n. 152, pp.574–5, 586–7.

[158] A. L. Goodhart, "The Imaginary Necktie and the Rule in *Re Polemis*" (1952) 68 *L.Q.R.* 514.

point that the decision did not square well with certain relevant precedents.[159] Secondly, he assessed the legacy of the decision, concluding that over thirty years it had "been cited in only a few cases, and . . . directly followed in only one".[160] Of course if the consequences of the decision really were, by and large, negligible, one might question why it deserved so much critical attention. For Goodhart, the answer to this question was straightforward: "the rule in *Re Polemis* . . . hangs like an albatross round the neck of anyone who may attempt to state in reasonably clear terms the general principles on which the law relating to damages is based".[161] Indeed, he added, "as long as *Re Polemis* survives it will be difficult to place the law of damages on a sound and reasonable foundation".[162]

Why did Goodhart believe this to be the case? For him, the primary flaw in the *Polemis* decision rested in the Court's insistence that tortfeasors be held liable for damage which, while not foreseeable, is "directly traceable to the negligent act".[163] What, he asked, is a direct consequence?

> "If X negligently leaves his horses unattended so that they run away when struck by a mischievous boy, and Y, a quarter of a mile away, is injured while attempting to stop them so as to save Z from harm, is Y's injury a direct consequence of X's negligence? . . . No one seems to have attempted a definition of the word 'direct' except to suggest that a cause continues to be direct until another intervenes. This seems to give us a clear mechanical test until we learn that an intervening cause is not an intervening cause if it ought to have been foreseen. X wounds Y, the wound becomes infected, and Y dies. Is the germ an intervening cause of Y's death? Is it an intervening cause if it was introduced intentionally or through the negligence of the hospital attendants? To suggest that the word *direct* can help us to answer such problems concerning responsibility is to ignore the fact that it has no precise meaning".[164]

The basic lesson of *Re Polemis*, for Goodhart, was that the law invariably evolves so much more satisfactorily when it follows the dic-

[159] See *ibid.*, pp.514–26. Like Pollock, Goodhart regarded *Hadley* v. *Baxendale* (1854) 9 Ex. 354 (a case which concerned damages for breach of contract as opposed to tortious liability) to be a particularly crucial sticking-point. Cf. F. P., Book Review (1928) 44 *L.Q.R.* 100 at 101–2.

[160] Goodhart, *supra* n. 158, p.530.

[161] *Ibid.*

[162] *Ibid.*, p.531.

[163] *Re Polemis*, *supra* n. 146, at 577 (per Scrutton LJ).

[164] Goodhart, *supra* n. 158, pp.530–1.

tates of experience rather than logic. "It is not unusual to find that in a conflict between law in practice on the one hand and attractive theory on the other, the ultimate victory goes to law in practice because experience has shown that it is based on a sounder and more workable principle".[165] When, in 1959, the Supreme Court of New South Wales handed down its decision in *The Wagon Mound*,[166] Goodhart declared that the time was ripe for judicial repudiation of *Re Polemis*.[167]

Repudiation came two years later, when *The Wagon Mound* was heard by the Judicial Committee of the Privy Council.[168] The case concerned the careless discharge into Sydney Harbour of a large quantity of furnace oil from the defendant's ship. The ship left the harbour around six hours after the spillage. The wind and tide carried the oil beneath the plaintiff's wharf where—the plaintiff having been advised that the activity remained safe—welding was being carried out. Some fifty-five to sixty hours after the spillage, molten metal from the welding operations fell from the wharf and set fire to some cotton waste or rag floating on the oil below. The waste set fire to the oil and a conflagration developed which seriously damaged the wharf. The oil also congealed upon and interfered with the plaintiff's use of the wharf's slipways. The defendants neither knew nor ought to have known that the oil was capable of being set alight when spread on water. Declining to follow *Re Polemis*, the Privy Council held that the defendants were not liable in negligence since they could not reasonably have foreseen that the plaintiff's wharf would be damaged by fire when they carelessly discharged oil into the harbour.

The Wagon Mound contains only one citation—indeed, a rather gratuitous citation—to Goodhart.[169] Yet this tells us next to nothing. Considerable portions of the reported decision may as well have come straight from Goodhart's pen, so accurately does the decision reflect his own views on *Re Polemis* and liability for consequences. Although counsel for the defendants made no reference to his campaign against the decision in *Polemis*, there seems little doubt that they were following what, in light of earlier discussion, we might term the Vaughan Williams philosophy: that counsel should refrain from citing living

[165] *Ibid.*, p.534.

[166] *Morts Dock & Engineering Co., Ltd.* v. *Overseas Tankship (U.K.) Ltd.* [1959] 2 Lloyd's Rep. 697.

[167] See Goodhart, *supra* n. 152, pp.585–7.

[168] *Overseas Tankship (U.K.) Ltd.* v. *Morts Dock & Engineering Co. Ltd. (The Wagon Mound)* [1961] AC 388.

[169] See *ibid.*, at 420–1 (per Viscount Simonds).

authors in court but feel free to appropriate their ideas. At length, for example, counsel endeavoured to demonstrate, just as had Goodhart, that "[t]he *Polemis* rule has . . . no pride of ancestry"[170] because the Court of Appeal, in arriving at the rule, had taken a decidedly selective approach to precedent. Far more significant than the arguments of counsel is the opinion of the Privy Council, which was delivered by Viscount Simonds. In 1955, Simonds had concluded one of his House of Lords opinions with an acknowledgement of indebtedness to Goodhart's scholarship.[171] The opinion in *The Wagon Mound* contains no such acknowledgement; but then it hardly needs to, for Goodhart's influence is evident on more or less every page. *Re Polemis*, Simonds argues, introduced into the law of negligence the idea "that the negligent actor is not responsible for consequences which are not 'direct', whatever that may mean".[172] The disparaging reference to the notion of direct consequences faintly echoes Goodhart. Returning to the issue of directness later on in the judgment, Simonds matches Goodhart almost word for word.[173] Why, Simonds asks, did the Court of Appeal reach the conclusion that it did as regards directness of consequences? "The answer appears to be that it was reached upon a consideration of certain authorities, comparatively few in number, that were cited to the court."[174] At this point, Simonds proceeds, as did counsel for the defendants, to rehearse the Goodhartian argument that *Re Polemis* sat uneasily *vis-à-vis* precedent and had rarely been followed in subsequent years.[175] Just as Goodhart had warned against judicial resort to "convoluted theorems", moreover, Simonds believed there to be a danger of courts "being led astray by scholastic theories of causation and their ugly and barely intelligible jargon".[176] Better to keep things simple: in determining the extent to which negligent

[170] *Overseas Tankship (U.K.) Ltd.* v. *Morts Dock & Engineering Co. Ltd. (The Wagon Mound)* [1961] AC 388 p.400, and see more generally *ibid.*, pp.394–401.

[171] *Benmax* v. *Austin Motor Co. Ltd.* [1955] AC 370, 374, per Viscount Simonds ("I ought not to conclude this opinion without saying how much I have owed in the preparation of it to certain writings by Professor Goodhart").

[172] *The Wagon Mound*, *supra* n. 168, at 416.

[173] *Ibid.*, at 424 ("The *Polemis* rule by substituting 'direct' for 'reasonably foreseeable' consequence leads to a conclusion equally illogical and unjust"); and cf. Goodhart, *supra* n. 152, p.587 ("*Polemis* solves no problems because it merely substitutes *direct* for *foreseeable*, as it is obvious that no one can be held liable for all the consequences of his wrongful acts").

[174] *The Wagon Mound*, *supra* n. 168, at 416.

[175] *Ibid.*, 416–22. That Pollock had disapproved of the decision, Simonds asserts, indicated "how far *Polemis* was out of the current of contemporary thought" (*ibid.*, at 420).

[176] *Ibid.*, at 419.

wrongdoers should be held responsible for the consequences of their actions, the most satisfactory test is that which "corresponds with the common conscience of mankind" rather than one "which leads to nowhere but the never-ending and insoluble problems of causation".[177] Goodhart had formulated what he considered to be the common sense proposition that tortfeasors should be held liable only for those consequences which a reasonable person would have foreseen as possible and would have avoided by due care. The decision of the Privy Council in *The Wagon Mound* very clearly embraces this proposition. According to Simonds:

> "[I]f it is asked why a man should be responsible for the natural or necessary or probable consequences of his act (or any other similar description of them) the answer is that it is not because they are natural or necessary or probable, but because, since they have this quality, it is judged by the standard of the reasonable man that he ought to have foreseen them".[178]

It seems no exaggeration to state that much of Viscount Simonds's opinion in *The Wagon Mound* is pure Goodhart. "The decision in the *Wagon Mound* is welcomed", J. A. Jolowicz quipped in the *Cambridge Law Journal* in 1961, "and it is reasonably foreseeable, at least to readers of the *Law Quarterly Review*, that even more enthusiastic receptions of the case may be forthcoming".[179] By that year, Goodhart believed, *Re Polemis* was dead and buried, and he was eager—perhaps too eager[180]—to dance on its grave. Contributing to the Notes section of the *Law Quarterly Review* an "obituary" on *Re Polemis*, he argued that the decision ought no longer to be regarded as authoritative notwithstanding that *The Wagon Mound*, being a decision of the Privy Council, was not binding on English courts and that the Court of Appeal was supposed to be bound by its own precedent. [181] There was little possibility that the House of Lords would reject the conclusion reached in *The Wagon Mound*: "it is probable that the same arguments which persuaded the Judicial Committee would be found to be valid

[177] *Ibid.*, at 423.

[178] *Ibid.*

[179] J. A. Jolowicz, "The Wagon Mound—A Further Comment" [1961] *C.L.J.* 30.

[180] See R. W. M. Dias, "Remoteness of Liability and Legal Policy" [1962] *C.L.J.* 178 at 180.

[181] See A. L. Goodhart, "Obituary: Re Polemis" (1961) 77 *L.Q.R.* 175 at 175–6; and cf. Glanville Williams, "The Risk Principle" (1961) 77 *L.Q.R.* 179 at 181 ("As a decision of the Privy Council, [*The Wagon Mound*] does not put the issue beyond all doubt. Although the Board purported to give *Re Polemis* its quietus . . . , the opinion does not take effect automatically for English law").

by the House of Lords. This, however, is a matter of opinion which cannot be discussed in a note".[182] Indeed, Goodhart ventured, "I believe that judicial statesmanship will lead to the conclusion that for all practical purposes *Re Polemis* is now dead, and that it is not necessary to wait for the House of Lords to administer the *coup de grâce*".[183] The *coup de grâce* was, in any event, not too long in coming.[184] Hardly surprisingly, it occasioned a celebratory case note by the editor of the *Law Quarterly Review*.[185]

As with Pollock, so too with Goodhart: citations to neither jurist capture the degree to which each was able to influence judicial decision-making at the highest levels. It was observed at the outset of this section that the eras of Pollock and Goodhart are sometimes characterized as antediluvian, as if it is really only in the last decades of the twentieth century that English judges became noticeably receptive to juristic opinion. Has history really evolved so straightforwardly? Perhaps, all things considered, it cannot but be right to assert that juristic thought became ever more of an influence over judicial decision-making as the twentieth century progressed. Yet it seems appropriate, in light of the preceding discussion of Pollock and Goodhart, to conclude this section by questioning whether the assertion might be simplistic.

When Pollock died in 1937, Birks has claimed, "things were not as they are now. The situation which we take for granted is a situation which is no older than the Second World War. Its final recognition is happening only now."[186] Birks is referring here to the vibrancy of academic law—"all those ever-multiplying journals, monographs and textbooks"[187]—and to the fact that, today, senior judges are prepared openly to discuss the merits of academic literature. He cites *Hunter* v. *Canary Wharf Ltd.*,[188] a case in which "two of their Lordships debated, and disagreed over, the proper use of academic literature", as possibly marking "the end of the beginning of the transformation of the common law".[189] As an illustration of judicial use of academic literature, the case is indeed interesting. Rather than debating and disagreeing

[182] Goodhart, *supra* n. 181, p.178.
[183] *Ibid.*, p.177; and cf. (1966) 82 *L.Q.R.* 444 at 448.
[184] *Hughes* v. *Lord Advocate* [1963] 2 WLR 779 (HL, Sc).
[185] (1964) 80 *L.Q.R.* 1; and see also (1962) 78 *L.Q.R.* 160; (1964) 80 *L.Q.R.* 145.
[186] Birks, *supra* n. 23, p.398.
[187] *Ibid.*
[188] *Hunter* v. *Canary Wharf Ltd.* [1997] 2 All ER 426 (HL).
[189] Birks, *supra* n. 23, p.398.

over the proper use of academic sources, two of their Lordships used different bodies of literature to reach different conclusions. In his dissenting opinion, Lord Cooke resorted to a line of academic commentary providing somewhat tentative support for the view that the right to sue in private nuisance in respect of interference with amenities should not be restricted to those with proprietary interests in the affected land.[190] Lord Goff, by contrast, relied on academic reasoning which supports the proposition that only those with rights in the affected land ought to be able to sue in private nuisance.[191] Although having consulted the literature used by Lord Cooke, Goff "did not, with all respect, find the stream of academic authority referred to . . . to be of assistance", since that literature provided "little more than an assertion of the desirability of extending the right of recovery" and "no analysis of the problem".[192]

At one level, Birks is very clearly right to shine the spotlight on *Hunter* v. *Canary Wharf*. The case is, after all, a high-profile decision of the House of Lords in which differences of judicial opinion turn to a significant extent on different readings of relevant academic literature. But is it right to say that the case epitomizes the final stages of a transformation in judicial attitudes towards juristic commentary, a transformation which had not begun at the time of Pollock's death and which really belongs to the second half of the last century? No doubt a transformation did occur. As was discussed earlier, the academic-legal profession has become so much larger, better organized and more of a presence *vis-à-vis* the legal profession generally. The appeal courts have, moreover, become less reluctant to acknowledge relevant juristic literature—although, as Birks concedes, the judicial decision which is explicitly reliant on such literature "is even now the exception rather than the rule".[193] The most difficult question to answer is whether the transformation which has occurred leads to the conclusion that juristic commentary is now more influential than it was during the eras of Pollock and Goodhart.

Perhaps this question has to be answered in the affirmative because the gradual relaxation of the convention against citation and the proliferation of academic lawyers and literature combine to determine that juristic influence must, nowadays, be more prevalent. Yet consider an

190 See *Hunter* v. *Canary Wharf*, *supra* n. 188, at 461–3.
191 See *ibid.*, at 434–41.
192 *Ibid.*, at 440–1.
193 Birks, *supra* n. 4, p.170.

alternative argument. The influence of both Pollock and Goodhart ran deep throughout the English appeal courts. Both were jurists in the lawyer-statesman mould—respected by, able to speak directly to and in fairly regular contact with the senior judiciary. The Matthew effect seemed to operate to the advantage of each: being creatures of a clubbish, conservative environment, judges of the Pollock and Goodhart eras would, in so far as they were prepared to listen to jurists at all, take heed or seek the opinion of only those jurists whose names were associated with sound judgment, common sense or whatever other qualities the judiciary cherished. The more often that Pollock and Goodhart provided advice which judges found valuable, the more inclined was the judiciary to take note of their advice.

During the eras of both men there were, admittedly, few if any other living jurists who would have been as respected and influential; yet it seems just as unlikely that more than a handful of modern English jurists would compare with either of them in this regard. There may (though this is by no means beyond question) be some modern academic lawyers who are more frequently cited in court, and there are certainly plenty of modern judicial opinions which draw attention to the influence of academic literature. That the influence of academic commentary has become more overt, however, does not mean that such commentary must nowadays be more influential. Most likely it now is more influential: explicit judicial regard for the opinions of numerous modern jurists certainly suggests as much. But we should hesitate to rush to this conclusion, not least because the judicial departures from *Derry* v. *Peek* and *Re Polemis* illustrate how, in the past, juristic influence could be peculiarly sustained and entrenched. It should be noted also that although certain modern academic lawyers have, in one way or another, succeeded in making a mark on judicial decision-making, they have tended to specialize in particular fields of law and it is difficult to say of any of them that they have been considerably more influential than were either Pollock or Goodhart.

The argument proffered here is not intended to romanticize the past. The point, rather, is that we ought to be wary about associating the past with inferiority. During the first half of the twentieth century, the academic-legal profession in England was something very different from what it is today. The way in which the profession, in so far as there was a profession, influenced judicial thinking throughout that period was also very different as compared with the present. The instances of academic influence in modern times are without doubt greater in number; yet when earlier judges were influenced by jurists, that influence would sometimes seem as if dyed into rather than laminated upon the relevant judgment. It is clear that, today, influence spreads wider. But it is not quite so obvious that it runs deeper.

MODERN TIMES

The argument which concludes the previous section might be summarized thus: in the past, judges were less often influenced by, and were less willing to acknowledge the influence of, jurists; yet when juristic ideas did find their way into judicial reasoning, it was sometimes because the ideas were considered so compelling as to determine what, as a matter of principle, the law should be. The implication is not that such academic influence is unknown in modern times, but that it would be a mistake to treat it as unique to modern times. The argument trades on a comparison of the past with the present; at the heart of the argument, indeed, is the idea that the phenomenon of juristic influence is not something new, that it is only the extent to and the ways in which the phenomenon is exhibited that have changed. The point of the argument is to try to say about the past something positive and oft-neglected. But it is easy to see how the argument might be misinterpreted as one of *plus ça change . . .*, as an effort to denigrate the present. We ought, therefore, to close this chapter with some discussion of the ways in which things have changed. What might be said about juristic influence in modern times? In what ways is the phenomenon manifested differently nowadays as compared with during the eras of Pollock and Goodhart?

Throughout the second half of the twentieth century, explicit acknowledgement of the potential value of juristic opinion became increasingly less unusual. Indeed, the case reports of that period attest to the fact that judges have become ever more willing to refer to jurists and their writings. It is worth noting also that, away from the courts, the founding of the Law Commission entailed the acknowledgement that academic lawyers have an important role to play in law reform. English Law Commissioners, section 1(2) of the Law Commissions Act 1965 stipulates, are to be chosen from "persons appearing to the Lord Chancellor to be suitably qualified by the holding of judicial office or by experience as a barrister or solicitor or as a teacher of law in a university".[194] With

[194] On academic appointments to the Law Commission in its early years, see J. H. Farrar, *Law Reform and the Law Commission* (London, Sweet & Maxwell, 1974),

the establishment of the Law Commission, Farrar wrote in 1974, the English legal system began to depend "more than ever before upon the work and active involvement of academic lawyers to write 'doctrine', initiate creative reform ideas, serve on or with reform bodies and measure the social effectiveness of law reform".[195]

During the last two decades of the century, academic lawyers began to discuss quite regularly the prospect of jurists and judges acting in partnership.[196] This discussion would have been fairly unremarkable were it not for the fact that it was primarily being encouraged by a senior judge. Lord Reid, as we saw earlier, had referred to the desirability of some sort of cooperative strategy in his address to the SPTL in 1972. His remarks, however, were essentially wishful-thinking, and offered little in the way of specifics. In *Spiliada* v. *Cansulex*, the case containing the citation which was deemed worthy of a circular at the LSE, Lord Goff concluded by:

> "paying tribute to the writings of jurists which have assisted me in the preparation of this opinion . . . I have not agreed with [these jurists] on all points but even when I have disagreed with them, I have found their work to be of assistance. For jurists are pilgrims with us on the endless road to unattainable perfection; and we have it on the excellent authority of Geoffrey Chaucer that conversations among pilgrims can be most rewarding".[197]

Goff spent the early part of the 1950s in academic life (before taking up practice at the commercial Bar) and has throughout his career been closely involved with law in the universities.[198] That he should have expressed such a sentiment, and that he should have reiterated it in other opinions,[199] is perhaps not surprising. More important than his voicing of the sentiment is the fact that he provided, in his Maccabaean Lecture of 1983, a down-to-earth assessment of how the partnership between judges and jurists ought to operate. Judges and jurists, he

pp.30–1, 41 n. 4. Academic lawyers are regularly appointed to the Commission to this day.

195 *Ibid.*, p.x.

196 See, e.g., Kötz, *supra* n. 4, p.190; Birks, *supra* n. 4, p.166; K. J. M. Smith, *Lawyers, Legislators and Theorists: Developments in English Criminal Jurisprudence 1800–1957* (Oxford, Clarendon Press, 1998), p.1; and Basil Markesinis, "Judicial Style and Judicial Reasoning in England and Germany" (2000) 59 *C.L.J.* 294 at 309.

197 *Spiliada* v. *Cansulex*, *supra* n. 2, at 488.

198 For details, see his entry in *Who's Who* and also Gareth Jones, "Lord Goff's Contribution to the Law of Restitution", in W. Swadling and G. Jones (eds), *The Search for Principle: Essays in Honour of Lord Goff of Chieveley* (Oxford, Oxford University Press, 1999), pp.207–33 at 207.

199 See, e.g., *Woolwich Equitable Building Society* v. *IRC* [1993] AC 70, 163–4 (HL).

observed, very obviously perform different tasks: whereas, "in the courts, single points of law are placed under the microscope",[200] jurists "adopt a much broader approach, concerned not so much with the decision of a particular case, but rather with the place of each decision in the law as a whole".[201] "[D]ifferent though judge and jurist may be, their work is complementary",[202] for "[t]he search for principle is a task which [they] share together".[203] While the formulation of legal principles is not as central to the role of most judges as it is to that of the jurist,[204] and although both groups tend to view principles differently—the judicial concern with principle tending to be less theoretical and more pragmatic[205]—the development of such principles is something "to which nowadays both judge and jurist contribute in . . . different ways".[206]

As between judge and jurist, however, whose view of principles ought to prevail? "[I]n . . . the development of legal principles", according to Goff, "the dominant power should . . . be that of the judge . . . because . . . the dominant element in the development of the law" should not be "theoretical development of legal principles"—"theories", after all, "are not necessarily drawn sufficiently widely or accurately to accommodate all . . . unforeseen and unforeseeable contingencies"—but "professional reaction to individual fact-situations".[207] For all that "[p]ragmatism must be the watchword", none the less, juristic preoccupation with principle is important: although "it is the judges who manufacture the tiny pieces of which the mosaic [of the law] is formed . . . [t]he jurists assess the quality of each piece so produced; they consider its place in the whole, and its likely effect in stimulating the production of new pieces, and the readjustment of others".[208] Not only is the juristic perspective important, it is becoming ever more influential:

[200] Robert Goff, "The Search for Principle" (1983) 69 *Proceedings of the British Academy* 169 at 185.

[201] *Ibid.*, p.184.

[202] *Ibid.*, p.171.

[203] *Ibid.*, p.187.

[204] See *ibid.*, pp.170–1.

[205] See *ibid.*, pp.184–7.

[206] *Ibid.*, p.172. Sometimes their contributions may overlap, as in the case of Robert Goff and Gareth Jones, *The Law of Restitution* (5th edn., London, Sweet & Maxwell, 1998; 1st edn. publ. 1966), and of *de Smith, Woolf & Jowell's Principles of Judicial Review* (London, Sweet & Maxwell, 1999).

[207] Goff, *supra* n. 200, pp.185–6; and see also The Right Hon. Lord Goff, "Judge, Jurist and Legislature" [1987] *Denning L. J.* 79 at 86–7.

[208] Goff, *supra* n. 200, p.186.

> "[T]he work of the judges has become more and more influenced by the teaching and writing of jurists. This influence is likely to continue to increase, especially as over three quarters of those entering the legal profession now read law for their degrees, and become exposed at their most impressionable and formative period to the influence of their teachers through their critical exposition of the principles of law".[209]

Modern judges are more likely to be influenced by the views of university lawyers, in other words, because, unlike in the past, their perspectives on law will probably have been formed at university. The style of a legal system, Weber believed, is to a significant degree determined by the manner in which its most prestigious lawyers (*Rechtshonoratioren*) are trained.[210] A system in which judges will have often worked as academics is more likely to breed a judiciary mindful of juristic critique. Within a system where judges for the most part acquire their training via the Bar, by contrast, the tendency to emphasize pragmatism while paying scant attention to what Goff calls the mosaic is likely to be more marked. To put the point somewhat crudely, the judge trained in university law is less likely to be indifferent to the opinions of university lawyers. "In the old days", Goff has observed, "it was not thought that law was a suitable subject for a liberal education; the best minds studied classical literature in the Latin and Greek languages, philosophy, ancient history". Nowadays, not only is law considered "an admirable subject for university study" but "[i]t is difficult to overestimate the influence of the jurist . . . both on the formation of the view of young lawyers and in the development of the law".[211]

When reflecting on Goff's remarks, it is worthwhile bearing in mind the unflattering opinions that certain judges had expressed about university lawyers in the past. If one holds up Goff's views against the backdrop of, say, those expressed by Devlin and Megarry, it should be fairly obvious why some modern academic lawyers have welcomed Goff's Maccabaean Lecture with open arms. Possibly the academic

[209] *Ibid.*, p.182.

[210] See Max Weber, *Economy and Society: An Outline of Interpretive Sociology*, 2 vols. (G. Roth and C. Wittich (eds), Eng. trans. E. Fischoff *et al.*, Berkeley, University of California Press, 1968 [1922]), II, pp.784–808; also Max Rheinstein, "Die Rechtshonoratioren und ihr Einfluß auf Charakter und Funktion der Rechtsordnungen" (1970) 34 *Rabels Zeitschrift für ausländisches und internationales Privatrecht* 1; and Konrad Zweigert and Hein Kötz, *Introduction to Comparative Law* (Eng. trans. T. Weir, 3rd edn., Oxford, Clarendon Press, 1998), pp.193–4.

[211] Goff, *supra* n. 207, p.92.

reception deserves to be treated with a degree of scepticism. Enthusiasm for the idea of a partnership between judge and jurist has come mainly from within those institutions to which appellate judges would be most likely to turn in seeking juristic opinion.[212] Away from Oxford, Cambridge and London, the idea seems to be received with a greater degree of indifference, in so far as it is received at all.[213] Institutions aside, there is also the question of whether jurists ought in any event to be trying to act in partnership with judges; there are those who would argue, that is, that legal scholarship produced with the concerns of judges in mind is likely to be intellectually compromised or unambitious.[214] Whether or not one shares such reservations, the fact is that Goff's views on jurists mark some sort of break with the past. Whereas, previously, the occasional judge had been known to make nice remarks about academics, or now and again cite the works of living jurists, or even do both of these things, Goff was different: first, because he endeavoured to explain both the value and limitations of juristic thought in relation to judicial decision-making; secondly, because his judgments, which regularly rely upon or engage with academic opinions,[215] demonstrate that he has practised what he has preached. Goff's confession that "I find it difficult to imagine how I could carry on my work without modern legal textbooks"[216] does not—as would be the case were these the words of almost any other judge—seem insincere.

[212] See, e.g., Birks, *supra* n. 4, pp.166–7; and cf. P. S. Atiyah, *Pragmatism and Theory in English Law* (London, Stevens & Sons, 1987), pp.183–4.

[213] An observation which was offered more than once in relation to an earlier draft of this chapter is that academics sometimes influence judges because judges seek their advice. Nicola Lacey, now at the London School of Economics, recalls that when she worked at New College, Oxford, she was struck "by the number of judges who turned up to law faculty dinners; some of them clearly had quite close intellectual relationships with law academics" (Nicola Lacey, e-mail to author, 6 March 2000.) Tony Honoré remarks similarly (letter to author, 20 August 2000) that "[q]uite a lot of academic influence takes place by way of judges asking their ex-tutors etc. what they think about so-and-so". Both Lacey and Honoré elaborate on these claims and, while Lacey is surely right when she observes that this particular form of influence tends to be "very hard to trace", various other correspondents reiterated the basic point. What is perhaps worth noting, notwithstanding that we would be silly to read much into the fact, is that all of the correspondents who did make this point are, or have been, academic lawyers at Oxford or Cambridge or in London.

[214] See, e.g., W. T. Murphy and Simon Roberts, "Introduction" (1987) 50 *M.L.R.* 677 at 679.

[215] For a fairly recent example, see *Kleinwort Benson Ltd.* v. *Lincoln City Council* [1998] 4 All ER 513, 541–3 (HL).

[216] Goff, *supra* n. 207, p.92.

For those who wish to know where the rub lies, this last observation marks the spot. How can it be said that the present differs much from the past if increased judicial appreciation of academic commentary is essentially attributable to one judge? It would be wrong to assume, in answer to the question, that Goff has been uniquely receptive. Lord Browne-Wilkinson effectively declared his support for the notion of partnership when, in *Linden Gardens* v. *Lenesta*, he asserted that the issue raised by the case "merits exposure to academic consideration before it is decided by this House"[217]—the implication being that judges may grapple better with novel or controversial legal issues when they can reflect upon how jurists have already approached such issues in the abstract. We noted earlier that when, in the early 1970s, Lord Denning expressed his disappointment with counsel for failing, in *White* v. *Blackmore*, to cite relevant academic commentary in the courtroom, he was rubbing against the grain of judicial convention. Today, his reproval would not be considered quite so radical. Over the past twelve years, failure of counsel to refer to relevant academic literature has been bemoaned by Lord Keith in *Rowling* v. *Takaro Properties*,[218] by Peter Gibson LJ in *State Bank of India* v. *Sood*[219] and by Lord Steyn in the Court of Appeal decision in *White* v. *Jones*.[220] In the latter case, the Court reconsidered the decision of Sir Robert Megarry V-C, in *Ross* v. *Caunters*, in which it was held that a solicitor who had been negligent in preparing a will could be liable to those who would otherwise have benefited under the will.[221] The appeal in *White* v. *Jones*, Steyn remarked:

> "lasted three days, and . . . we were referred to about forty decisions of English and foreign courts. Pages and pages were read from some of the judgments. But we were not referred to a single piece of academic writing on *Ross v Caunters*. Counsel are not to blame: traditionally counsel make very little use of academic materials other than standard textbooks. In a difficult case it is helpful to consider academic comment on the point. Often such writings examine the history of the problem, the framework into which a decision must fit and countervailing policy considerations in greater depth than is usually possible in judgments prepared by judges who are faced with a remorseless treadmill of cases that cannot wait. And it is arguments that influence decisions rather than the reading of pages upon pages from judg-

[217] *Linden Gardens Trust Ltd* v. *Lenesta Sludge Disposals Ltd.* [1994] AC 85, 112.
[218] *Rowling* v. *Takaro Properties Ltd* [1988] AC 473, 500 (PC).
[219] *State Bank of India* v. *Sood* [1997] Ch. 276, 281, 285 (CA).
[220] *White* v. *Jones* [1993] 3 All ER 481 (CA).
[221] *Ross* v. *Caunters* [1980] Ch. 297.

ments . . . [Academic] material, properly used, can sometimes help to give one a better insight into the substantive arguments . . . [T]he arguments for and against the ruling in *Ross v Caunters* were clarified for me by academic writings".[222]

The sentiment encapsulated in this passage is, of course, familiar to us. That academic commentary can aid judicial deliberation is an idea which, as we saw above, was supported by English judges of an earlier era. But those judges were perhaps not as receptive to such literature as are certain of their modern counterparts. In *White* v. *Jones*, for example, Steyn not only refers to a significant body of academic literature but proceeds, in his judgment, to illustrate the relevance of that literature to his own position on the liability of solicitors to disappointed beneficiaries.[223] In many ways, the past and the present seem hardly different: judicial acknowledgement of the value of academic commentary is no more a peculiarly late-twentieth century phenomenon than is juristic influence over judicial decision-making. In so far as a difference does exist, however, it seems to rest in the detail: as compared with earlier judges who were receptive to academic opinion, certain modern judges of essentially the same disposition seem more willing not only to acknowledge that juristic views have influenced them, but also to try to indicate the nature of the influence—or even, where relevant academic commentary has not influenced them, to explain why this should be the case. Just as juristic influence is not something new, so too its contours have not remained unchanged.

222 *White* v. *Jones*, *supra* n. 220, at 500; and cf. Werner Lorenz and Basil Markesinis, "Solicitors' Liability Towards Third Parties: Back Into the Troubled Waters of the Contract/Tort Divide" (1993) 56 *M.L.R.* 558 at 563. This last piece, a case note dealing with the Court of Appeal's decision in *White* v. *Jones*, illustrates how case note writing is sometimes conceived to be a normative activity. At the time that it was written, the Case Notes Editor of the *Modern Law Review*, Roger Brownsword, operated a policy of "hold[ing] off commenting on cases before the appeals had been completed (waiting until after the HL decision if necessary)". However, the authors of this particular case note were "very keen to get a comment on the CA decision in *White* v. *Jones* into print before the HL heard the appeal" because they "clearly felt that their note might make a difference". Brownsword concedes that his policy until that point "might have been misguided. In other words, I might have assumed incorrectly that the function of the case note was to offer ex post reflection on a case (largely for the benefit of the academic community) rather than to intervene in a case during its passage through the courts": Roger Brownsword, letter to author, 26 May 1999. Although Lorenz's and Markesinis's case note makes no appearance in the House of Lords' decision in *White* v. *Jones*, certain of their other writings do: see *White* v. *Jones*, *supra* n. 95, at 705–8 (per Lord Goff).

223 See *White* v. *Jones*, *supra* n. 220, at 500–3. By contrast, in his House of Lords judgment in this case Lord Goff cites academic literature primarily for the purpose of disagreeing with it: see *White* v. *Jones*, *supra* n. 95, at 705–8.

It is tempting to speculate that juristic opinion will become ever more influential in the courtroom as the law becomes increasingly complex. It would not be altogether surprising were we to witness greater judicial reliance on academic commentary with the incorporation into English law of much of the European Convention on Human Rights under the Human Rights Act 1998. Reliance on academic opinion when tackling complex legal problems is very much a feature of private international law: that is, in conflict of laws cases where a party seeks to prove foreign law the court must receive expert evidence with regard to the relevant rules. Not surprisingly, this evidence will quite often be provided by an academic lawyer.[224] An empirical study published in 1990 provides limited support for the proposition that English judges are more likely to rely on academic commentaries when deciding cases which do not fall squarely within, and which demand knowledge extending significantly beyond, the more traditional legal categories.[225] Medical law would seem to be a case in point. When deciding cases revolving around issues of medical ethics—determining when life support should be withdrawn, for example, or when a patient should be denied the right to refuse medical treatment—appellate judges are possibly more inclined than they would otherwise be to introduce academic opinions (though not always academic-legal opinions) into their judgments.[226] We ought, however, to be wary of such speculation. Without data facilitating comparisons of judicial use of academic literature as between different areas of law, it is not especially helpful. Indeed, speculation along these lines is somewhat undermined by the fact that, throughout the second half of the last century, it is in one of the most traditional areas of law that academic commentary has been consistently and noticeably influential: anyone seeking to appreciate the capacity of jurists to influence judges in modern times is unlikely to discover any more appropriate area of study than the criminal law.

It was during the years following the Second World War, Smith has argued, that criminal law scholarship came into its own in the English

[224] See generally *Dicey and Morris on the Conflict of Laws*, 2 vols. (L. Collins *et al.* (eds), 13th edn., London, Sweet & Maxwell, 2000), I, pp.225–7.

[225] Peter Clinch, "The Use of Authority: Citation Patterns in the English Courts" (1990) 46 *Jnl. of Documentation* 287 at 315.

[226] See, e.g., *Re W (A Minor) (Medical Treatment)* [1993] Fam. 64, 75, CA (per Lord Donaldson MR); *Airedale N.H.S. Trust* v. *Bland* [1993] 1 All ER 821 (Fam. D, CA and HL).

courtroom.[227] To document exhaustively the impact of such scholarship on judicial thought would probably require the length of this present chapter again, and so the following discussion offers but a few illustrations of how, in modern times, juristic critique has proved influential. At the risk of over-emphasizing the medium, it is worth noting once more the significance of the case note. As any English lawyer knows, not all case notes are of the same type. Such notes differ in length and style from one journal to the next. Some journals specialize in narrowly-focused doctrinal notes, written for (and often by) practising lawyers. Others publish more ambitious commentaries, often the product of distinguished academics. Some publish something in between, or a mixture of, the two styles. Some journals produce only two or three issues per year, which means that the notes in those journals often appear after relevant decisions have been heard on appeal; some produce six or more issues each year, which may increase the likelihood of notes appearing before the appeals are heard. The *Criminal Law Review* appears monthly and contains a section in which recent criminal cases are reported in summary and subjected to brief commentary. Since the cases and commentaries are juxtaposed, since both are short (ensuring that a large number of case notes can be packed into each issue of the journal) and since the commentaries often appear before relevant cases go to appeal, the *Criminal Law Review* might be said to respond fairly efficiently to the decision-making process: indeed, the journal's case note format is rather akin to that which has traditionally prevailed in France (see Chapter 4).

In 1956, two years after the *Criminal Law Review* was established, J. C. Smith was appointed as the journal's commentary writer. He remains as one of the journal's commentary team to this day. "I make no apologies", he wrote in 1980:

> "for having devoted to this task a substantial amount of time which might otherwise have been spent in producing articles or a book. I believe it to be worthwhile because the Review's message gets through, and gets through quickly, not only to teachers and students but also to many of those engaged in the practice of the law—police, solicitors, barristers and judges".[228]

Smith's own commentaries are regularly referred to in appellate judgments, and can be seen to have influenced the path of the criminal

[227] See Smith, *supra* n. 196, pp.369–78.

[228] J. C. Smith, "An Academic Lawyer and Law Reform" (1981) 1 *Legal Studies* 119 at 120–1. (The article is the text of Smith's Presidential address to the SPTL, delivered in September 1980.)

law over the years.[229] That this is the case can perhaps be deduced from the following three illustrations. First of all, in *Preddy*[230] (a case concerning acquisition of property by deception contrary to section 15(1) of the Theft Act 1968) the House of Lords discredited the Court of Appeal's decision in *Halai*.[231] Delivering the main judgment in *Preddy*, Lord Goff declared himself unconvinced by Smith's criticisms of the outcome of the case in the Court of Appeal[232] but believed there to be "considerable force" to his critique of *Halai*.[233] Goff also relied on Smith's commentaries on two other Court of Appeal decisions, *Mitchell* and *Duru*, in order to demonstrate the extent to which both were wrongly decided.[234] Secondly, the *Criminal Law Review* published in 1978 a summary of the Court of Appeal's decision in *Hussein*, a case which concerned the notion of "conditional intention" in theft. The Court held that such intent was insufficient to establish criminal liability: "it cannot be said that one who has it in his mind to steal only if what he finds is worth stealing has a present intention to steal".[235] If this decision were correct, Smith commented, those who enter buildings intending to steal nothing specific but only whatever they find to be valuable cannot be said to have a present intention to steal.[236] Such a decision, in short, "could be the burglars' charter".[237] Although the Court of Appeal subsequently claimed that Smith had misunderstood the implications of *Hussein* owing to the fact that certain crucial details had been omitted from the law reports,[238] the Law Commission in 1979 instigated Attorney General's References[239] in order that the law concerning conditional intention to steal, which, it was conceded, *Hussein* had rendered "a little elliptical",[240] be made clearer. Thirdly, in

[229] The shelf-life of Smith's commentaries is perhaps shorter than that of many other case notes owing to the fact that the commentaries are often incorporated into the latest edition of his *The Law of Theft* or Smith and Hogan's *Criminal Law*. Once so incorporated, the courts tend to refer to the relevant textbook rather than to the original commentaries.

[230] *R.* v. *Preddy* [1996] AC 815.

[231] *R.* v. *Halai* [1983] Crim. LR 624.

[232] *R.* v. *Preddy*, *supra* n. 230, at 834; and see also [1995] Crim. LR 565–6.

[233] *R.* v. *Preddy* at 840; and see also [1983] Crim. LR 626.

[234] See *R.* v. *Preddy* at 836–7.

[235] *R.* v. *Husseyn (Note)* (1978) 67 Cr. App. R. 131, 132 (per Lord Scarman); [1978] Crim. LR 219 (*sub nom. Hussein*).

[236] [1978] Crim. LR 219.

[237] *Ibid.*, at 220.

[238] See Smith, *supra* n. 228, pp.121–2.

[239] See *Law Commission, 14th Annual Report, 1978–79* (House of Commons, 16 January 1980), p.11.

[240] *Attorney-General's References (Nos. 1 and 2 of 1979)* [1979] 3 WLR 577, 586.

Anderton v. *Ryan* the House of Lords interpreted section 1 of the Criminal Attempts Act 1981 to mean that a defendant cannot be guilty of an attempt to commit an offence where the crime in question cannot be completed: hence, a person who mistakenly believes property to be stolen, and who receives the property on that basis, could not be guilty of attempting to handle stolen goods.[241] Section 1(2) of the 1981 Act states unequivocally that "[a] person may be guilty of attempting to commit an offence [of handling stolen goods] even though the facts are such that the commission of the offence is impossible". "The Law Commission recommended this legislation", Glanville Williams memorably observed, "because experience showed that the whole subject was an intellectual minefield; so the only thing to do was to fence it off and erect a 'Keep out' notice, to prevent the courts from continuing to make asses of themselves".[242] When the House of Lords failed to heed the warning, Smith produced a commentary which pulled no punches:

> "The House of Lords has done it again. Confusion and uncertainty have been substituted for the orderly and simple solution of this long-standing problem intended by Parliament . . . This is a dangerous area in which to rely on arguments from absurdity; and their Lordships obligingly provide their critics with ample ammunition to demonstrate the morass in which they have landed us . . . The task must now be to see what can be salvaged from the wreck of the Law Commission's and Parliament's intentions".[243]

In *Shivpuri*, the House of Lords overturned *Anderton* v. *Ryan*. Lord Bridge (who managed to be in the majority in both cases!) criticized *Anderton* v. *Ryan* by employing reasoning and analogies which had been used in Smith's commentary.[244] More obviously influential was Glanville Williams, who had campaigned hard for the abolition of the defence of impossibility and who regarded *Anderton* v. *Ryan* with a mixture of incredulity and disdain.[245] "I cannot conclude this opinion", Lord Bridge, famously remarked:

> "without disclosing that I have had the advantage, since the conclusion of the argument in this appeal, of reading an article by Professor Glanville Williams entitled "The Lords and Impossible Attempts, or Quis Custodiet Ipsos Custodies [*sic*]?" [1986] CLJ 33. The language in which he criticises the

[241] *Anderton* v. *Ryan* [1985] AC 560.
[242] Glanville Williams, "The Lords and Impossible Attempts, or *Quis Custodiet Ipsos Custodes*?" (1986) 45 *C.L.J.* 33 at 38.
[243] [1985] Crim. LR 504 at 504–5.
[244] Cf. *R.* v. *Shivpuri* [1986] 2 All ER 334, 344–5; and *supra* n. 243 at 506.
[245] See Williams, *supra* n. 242, *passim*; also Atiyah, *supra* n. 212, pp.180–2.

decision in *Anderton v Ryan* is not conspicuous for its moderation, but it would be foolish, on that account, not to recognise the force of the criticism and churlish not to acknowledge the assistance I have derived from it".[246]

This account could easily be extended with illustrations of how Williams, like Smith, was able to influence significantly the development of the criminal law.[247] It could be prolonged still further were we to assess the considerable influence on the criminal law of certain contemporary jurists,[248] and, of course, further again were we to look beyond the criminal law. But it is hoped that enough has been done to demonstrate the capacity of modern academic commentary to influence judicial decision-making. More general discussions of the relationship in modern times between academics and judges—and, more broadly still, between academics and practitioners—have been undertaken by others, and there seems little point in extending this chapter simply by repeating their findings. About these studies, however, we might observe that there are subtle differences in argument. Some commentators are, not without reason, inclined to accentuate the negative, to emphasize that although, during the past century, the relationship between the academic and the practitioner (including the courts) grew closer, there still exists between the two groups a significant divide—a divide which is in danger of widening.[249] Others preach cautious optimism, arguing that although there are indications that juristic influence is becoming more widespread, there remains a tendency for many, if not the majority of, judges and legal practitioners

[246] *R.* v. *Shivpuri*, *supra* n. 244, at 345. Williams's article had apparently been toned down on editorial advice! See A. T. H. Smith, "Glanville Williams: Police Powers and Public Law" (1997) 56 *C.L.J.* 462 at 464.

[247] For those seeking such illustrations, see Smith, *supra* n. 196, pp.304–60; Atiyah, *supra* n. 212, pp.181–3; John Smith, "The Sad Fate of the Theft Act 1968", in *The Search for Principle*, *supra* n. 198, pp.97–113; P. R. Glazebrook, "Glanville Williams: Criminal Law" (1997) 56 *C.L.J.* 445; J. R. Spencer, "Glanville Williams: Criminal Procedure and Evidence" (1997) 56 *C.L.J.* 456; and Andrew Grubb, "Glanville Williams: A Personal Appreciation" (1998) 6 *Medical L. Rev.* 133 at 135–6. I have focused on Smith instead of Williams because Smith's contribution to the development of the criminal law seems to illustrate particularly well the influential role of the case note.

[248] See, e.g., *Luc Thiet Thuan* v. *The Queen* [1996] 2 All ER 1033, 1041, per Lord Goff (PC); and also the judgments of Lord Clyde, Lord Millett, Lord Hobhouse and, especially, Lord Hoffmann in *R.* v. *Smith* [2000] 3 WLR 654 (HL).

[249] See, in particular, Birks, *supra* n. 4, pp.170–9; *supra* n. 23, pp.402–14. A still less optimistic (and to my mind unconvincing) argument, developed specifically in relation to English jurisprudence, is advanced by Cosgrove: see Richard A. Cosgrove, *Scholars of the Law: English Jurisprudence from Blackstone to Hart* (New York, New York University Press, 1996); and cf. Neil Duxbury, "The Narrowing of English Jurisprudence" (1997) 95 *Michigan L. Rev.* 1990.

to ignore academic research.[250] Others are less cautiously optimistic, particularly with regard to the bonds forged between academic and practising lawyers.[251] The primary purpose of this chapter, by contrast with these studies, has not been to predict the future but to analyse history. The relationship between jurist and judge in England has been peculiar, complex and difficult to fathom. That certain modern judges are more willing than were their predecessors to acknowledge juristic influence does not mean that such influence is a modern phenomenon. It merely means that influence is now less difficult to detect. My main objective here has been to cast some light on a somewhat shrouded past: on the relationship, that is, between jurist and judge before the citation of academic commentary in court became more or less respectable.

CONCLUSION

Doom and gloom abounds. "English academic writings are rarely cited to the courts, and carry little weight where they are cited."[252] "None [of the various forms of legal scholarship] is likely to carry great weight when compared with the products of other disciplines or even the works of legal scholarship in other countries."[253] As for the case note:

> "what end is in view? And what is achieved at the end of the day? The cases are in place, for the moment; the regulations are in order, just for now; but the relationship to 'now' is in the hands of others . . . so a casenote is concluded by writing that 'It is to be hoped that the House of Lords will be able to review this branch of the law at the earliest opportunity.' Words, with greater or less effort, fill the page, fill the world: to what end, to what avail? I have often wished that I knew the answers to such questions".[254]

[250] See, e.g., Geoffrey Wilson, "English Legal Scholarship" (1987) 50 *M.L.R.* 818 at 842–3; B. S. Markesinis, "A Matter of Style" (1994) 110 *L.Q.R.* 607 at 621–3.

[251] See, e.g., Martin Partington, "Academic Lawyers and 'Legal Practice' in Britain: A Preliminary Reappraisal" (1988) 15 *Jnl. Law & Soc.* 374; "Academic Lawyers and Legal Practice in England: Towards a New Relationship?" (1992) 3 *Legal Education Review* 75; and cf. also Andrew Halpin, "Law, Theory and Practice: Conflicting Perspectives?", in A. Sherr and D. Sugarman (eds), *Theory in Legal Education* (Aldershot, Ashgate, forthcoming).

[252] P. S. Atiyah and R. S. Summers, *Form and Substance in Anglo-American Law: A Comparative Study of Legal Reasoning, Legal Theory, and Legal Institutions* (Oxford, Clarendon Press, 1987), p.403.

[253] Wilson, *supra* n. 250, p.818.

[254] W. T. Murphy, "Reference Without Reality: A Comment on a Commentary on Codifications of Practice" (1990) 1 *Law and Critique* 61 at 74 n. 14.

No doubt a good deal of academic commentary does fall by the wayside. Indeed, as was noted in Chapter 2, legal scholarship is a high-risk, low return activity. Perhaps, in England, the returns are no lower than might be expected. We have seen that academic writings can carry considerable weight in court and that even case notes sometimes influence appellate decisions. Few academics have produced works as influential as certain of those by Pollock, Goodhart, J. C. Smith and Glanville Williams. That the achievements of these men were exceptional, however, does not imply that they held a monopoly over juristic influence. Why should any academic lawyer wish to offer unsolicited advice to courts? Aside from the imperative to publish, there is the encouragement that might be discerned from history: those academics with any awareness of the relationship between jurists and judges in England over the past century or so are likely to reach the conclusion that the advice that they offer, for all that it is unlikely to be acknowledged, might just reach the desired audience.

Note that the doom and gloom that does abound is the product of academic lawyers. Perhaps it is not wholly flippant to suggest that the status of the English jurist will have been well and truly raised not when more judges begin to emulate Robert Goff, but when they begin to articulate disappointment in the style of Harry Edwards (see Chapter 3). The image of an English judge expressing concern that too many jurists are ignoring the needs of practitioners and judges is perhaps too futuristic for some. It may, however, be closer to the present than we realize.[255] While there remain significant differences between the higher courts in the USA and England, it is worth noting both that the House of Lords now makes use of research assistants and that the English appellate judge with an academic career to his or her name is no longer a rarity. Not only, furthermore, is the higher judiciary now much larger in number than during the eras of either Pollock or Goodhart, but it is probably the case that fewer barristers appointed today as High Court judges will have the experience of general practice that would once have been common. Given the growth and complexity of modern law and the increased likelihood of judges having to decide legal issues which fall outside their own areas of expertise, it is perhaps not surprising that the overt use of academic commentary in

[255] Consider the lament of one academic lawyer and Law Commissioner: Andrew Burrows, "Restitution: Where Do We Go From Here?" (1997) 50 *C.L.P.* 95 at 109–11, 115–17; repr. in his *Understanding the Law of Obligations: Essays on Contract, Tort and Restitution* (Oxford, Hart, 1998), pp.99–119 at 112–14, 118–19.

legal judgments should have increased fairly dramatically over the past three decades. The day when English judges feel slighted by jurists, rather than jurists by judges, is not entirely beyond the imagination.

In the latter stages of this chapter there has evolved a sub-plot of sorts concerning juristic influence in modern times as compared with during the eras of Pollock and Goodhart. Whatever one makes of this sub-plot—whether or not one agrees that it may be simplistic to argue that juristic influence is greater today than it used to be—it ought not to detract from the main storyline: that comparisons of the significance accorded by courts to academic commentary often neglect the fact that influence tends to manifest itself differently from one jurisdiction to next. It seems hardly surprising to find academic lawyers arguing that jurists in England have not been as successful as have their continental and American counterparts in influencing the work of the courts. Yet this argument, for all that it seems unsurprising, is difficult to sustain. Even the most formidable legal intellect would struggle to argue convincingly that juristic opinion has exerted a greater influence over judicial thought in England than it has in the USA or France.[256] At the heart of this book rests a less ambitious (but still, I hope, contentious) claim: that an analysis of the relationship between jurist and judge within each jurisdiction shows it to be far from clear that academic lawyers have been more influential in the USA and France than has been the case in England.

[256] Though for the argument that as English jurists become ever more influential, their American counterparts become ever less so, see John H. Langbein, "Scholarly and Professional Objectives in Legal Education: American Trends and English Comparisons", in P. B. H. Birks (ed.), *Pressing Problems in the Law, Volume 2: What Are Law Schools For?* (Oxford, Oxford University Press, 1996), pp.1–7 at 3–6; and also, in a similar vein, Reinhard Zimmermann, "Savigny's Legacy: Legal History, Comparative Law, and the Emergence of a European Legal Science" (1996) 112 *L.Q.R.* 576 at 583–4.

6

Envoi

THIS BOOK HAS considered the influence of jurists on judges. Its scope has been rather narrow and its methodology somewhat haphazard. We have examined only three jurisdictions and have taken a very selective approach to the literature within those jurisdictions. More has been said about England than about either the USA or France, and in considering each jurisdiction our focal point has varied. The discussion of scholarship and the courts in the USA focused more or less exclusively on the student-edited law school review as seen through the eyes of both judges and academics. Our reflections on France centred on the history and the influence of the *note d'ârret* or case note. The case note featured fairly prominently in our account of juristic influence in England, too, although there we considered in far more detail than we did in relation to either the USA or France the relationship between jurist and judge. This unevenness of treatment reflects to a significant extent the differing degrees to which, within each jurisdiction, academics and judges have themselves reflected and commented on the subject of juristic influence. While I consider disparity of treatment as between the three jurisdictions studied to be inevitable, I also consider it, certainly for the purposes of this project, to be irrelevant. The general objective of this book has been to caution against broad intra-jurisdictional comparisons of juristic influence; the more specific objective has been to try to demonstrate that propositions to the effect that English academic lawyers are less influential than are their continental and North American counterparts invariably deserve (appropriating a phrase from Holmes) to be washed with cynical acid. I hope that enough has been done here in support of both of these objectives.

The one thing that ought to be clear, whatever one makes of this book and its objectives, is that there are much bigger fish to fry. While we have been concerned here with little more than the identification of juristic influence, a far more ambitious study would endeavour to determine what types of influences jurists have sought to exert. Throughout the history of English law, for example, what sorts of things have jurists been saying to the courts and the legal profession? What have been their expectations of judges, legislators and practitioners? What have they wanted them to do? Do we find academic lawyers relying on a distinct repertoire of arguments, tropes and conclusions? How deep, furthermore, runs that feeling of academic frustration which we adverted to in the Preface and glimpsed in the last chapter? Simply to study the academic lawyer as a critic of judicial decisions, which is more or less all that we have done here, will not furnish us with answers to these questions. We need also studies of the development of legal scholarship and textbook writing more generally, of the arguments and normative agenda developed and advanced by legal academics, of the roles played by these academics, of their objectives and achievements as scholars, teachers and legal consultants; in short, we need to delve deeper into the history and development of law as an academic discipline in England. Some of this work, as was noted in the Preface, has already been done. But there is a long way to go yet. This book is but a footstep on that formidable journey.

Index

American legal realism, 40
  arrêtistes, 49–54, 56–7

Brandeis, Louis, 25–7

Cardozo, Benjamin, 24–5, 27, 30–1
case notes, 3, 113–17
  in America, 23, 56
  in England, 54–6, 85–7, 91–8
  in English criminal law, 109–12
  in France, 48–59, 109
citation, 1–2, 8–17, 33–7, 61
  in English courts, convention against, 62–84
  motives for, 9–12
  relationship with influence, 12–17, 22, 84
conflict of laws, 108
criminal law scholarship, 108–13

declaratory theory of law, 66–7
Denning, Alfred, 78–81, 88, 106
Devlin, Patrick, 1, 74, 81, 89, 104
doctrinal scholarship, 42–5

Edwards, Harry, 24, 31–2, 43–5, 114
exegetical school, 51

Goff, Robert, 99, 102–6, 110, 114
Goodhart, Arthur, 19, 82–3, 87–101, 114–15

Holmes, Oliver Wendell, 11, 30, 117

incommensurability, 2, 117
influence, 2–3, 5–22, *passim*
  elusiveness of, 17–22
  juristic, 54–9, 87, 90, 98–101, 103–8, 115
  literary theory and, 6–7

law and economics, 39
law clerks, 20–1, 36–7
Law Commission, 101–2
law reviews:
  American, 27–33
  English, 61, 109
  French, 56–7
legal academics:
  American, 23, 38–46
  English, 74–7, 101–2
  French, 56–9
legal research, 69–73

Matthew Effect, 11–12, 14, 18, 35–6, 43, 100
medical law, 108
Megarry, Robert, 67, 74–6, 104

normative legal scholarship, 38
  redundancy of, 39–40

oral judicial tradition, 67–8

partnership:
  jurists and judges, between, 81–2, 102–5, 112–13
Pollock, Frederick, 19, 52, 65, 70, 78, 84–7, 92, 98–101, 114–15
Posner, Richard, 5–6, 31–2

Rechtshonoratioren, 104
Roman law, 48–9

Smith, J. C., 109–12, 114

Traynor, Roger, 28, 35, 37

Williams, Glanville, 111–12, 114